What is Christmas?
It is the tenderness of the past,
courage for the present, and hope for the future.

—Agnes M. Pahro

Sweet Carolina
MYSTERIES

Sweet ✦ Carolina

MYSTERIES

'TWAS THE CLUE BEFORE CHRISTMAS

Tia McCollors

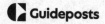

'TWAS THE CLUE BEFORE CHRISTMAS

Chapter One

I**T WAS BEGINNING TO LOOK** a lot like Christmas at the Bashore house. Despite the consistently mild temperatures that Charleston residents had been enjoying for the month, Shirley knew that her mother had one purpose and one purpose only when she arose on this sunshiny Saturday morning—to transform their home into a winter wonderland.

Groggy and eyes half-closed, Shirley plodded to the kitchen for a cup of morning coffee and nearly stumbled over the sealed cardboard box left haphazardly in the hallway.

"Goodness gracious," she moaned, her voice still raspy with sleep. "I know what this means." Shirley eyed the box marked O**RNAMENTS** and noticed the others that had been pushed into a corner of their quaint living room. Her father's prized Christmas train, which puffed real smoke, sat on the coffee table, still in its original box and packed tightly in Styrofoam. Thinking of the look on her father's face as the train *choo-chooed* around the perimeter of their live Christmas tree gave Shirley a warm and fuzzy feeling. Her father had always loved this time of year.

The handcrafted porcelain village that Shirley's mother meticulously sealed in bubble wrap at the end of each holiday season had been placed in its customary spot on the fireplace mantel. At night, some of the snow-capped houses emitted a soft amber glow thanks to the miniature electric bulbs inside. And in place of the stack of coasters on the coffee table was a handcrafted wooden nativity scene. It was the same every year. With her mother's fading memories, Shirley was grateful for every memory that was still within her grasp.

"You've been busy this morning," Shirley said as her mother rounded the corner from the kitchen. "Very busy."

"When I wake up after dreaming about sugarplums, then I figure it's about time."

"I'm glad you've had sweet dreams. Most of the time I'm dreaming about my patients or something happening at Mercy Hospital. It's been extremely busy over the last couple of months."

"Then tonight will be a nice change of pace," Mama added. "I've been wanting to get all fancy and glitzy for a while."

"I know you have," Shirley said, laughing. She pulled a bag of roasted coffee beans from the cabinet. "Maybe you should go in my place. I'll stay behind this evening and—I don't know—unpack your angel figurines."

"You'll do no such thing," Mama said.

When her mother crossed her arms, Shirley knew she meant business. "You are a special guest tonight and if anyone needs to be there, it's you. Mr. Christmas took a special liking to you. He probably would've stolen you from me as his own daughter if he could."

"I don't know what it was about him, but we clicked like we'd known each other for years. I'm going to miss him and his jolly personality. He could light up an entire room like a tree full of sparkling holiday lights."

"I've always heard about the annual party at the Christmas mansion. Thanks for letting me come along."

Shirley smirked. "Garrison wouldn't have it any other way."

Garrison Baker, Shirley's beau, would be accompanying them to the evening's festivities at the home of the late Mr. Benjamin Christmas. For as long as Shirley could remember, Mr. Christmas had hosted a party to kick off the holiday tour of homes in his wealthy and historic Charleston neighborhood. The ninety-three-year-old man had loved the holiday and spent his entire life spreading the kind of joy and cheer that was synonymous with his name. During his extended stay at Mercy Hospital over the final months of his illness, he insisted that some of the staff and employees he'd grown to love attend his traditional party—regardless of whether he'd be there to enjoy it with him.

"The show must go on. Whether I'm on this earth or at my heavenly home," Shirley remembered him saying.

She had made it a point to slip into his private room at least once during her shift, even if the visit lasted just a few minutes. Over the weeks and months, those moments grew into meaningful time spent together. During Shirley's last visit with Mr. Christmas, he didn't have the strength to speak, yet his eyes fluttered open for a moment at the sound of her voice. That same night he slipped away peacefully during his sleep. Shirley had known the time was imminent, but when she heard the news her heart ached in a way that she hadn't expected.

She would honor him with her attendance tonight, although the experience would be bittersweet.

Shirley spent the majority of the day resting, since her mother had always been particular about the arrangement of her Christmas decor and insisted that she didn't need her daughter's assistance. So Shirley kept out of the way, propped her feet up, and binge-watched cooking and home improvement shows until it was time to kick off her bedroom slippers and step into her high heels.

"How long before Garrison arrives?" Mama asked. She draped a glittery shawl around her shoulders, which she pinned in place with an oversized poinsettia pin with red leaves trimmed in gold.

"He should be here shortly," Shirley said.

"I would hope so," Mama said. "He's always a timely man. Except when it comes to matters of marriage and proposals. He's taking a little too long for my taste." She settled into her favorite chair and perched her purse on her lap. "But I know my future son-in-law won't keep me—or you—waiting long." She batted her eyes. "Hopefully."

"Mama," Shirley fussed. "You know calling Garrison that is against the rules."

"Against whose rules?"

"Mine," Shirley said, crossing her arms in overexaggerated annoyance. "It's no secret that I care for Garrison as much as he cares for me, but there's no sense in trying to rush us down the aisle."

"Neither one of you is a spring chicken." Mama shrugged. "I'm merely stating the obvious. When you're up in age it doesn't take that long to know what you want. Or *who* you want."

"If it's to be, then it's all in God's timing," Shirley said. She slipped in a pair of dangly gold earrings and admired herself in the hallway mirror. Stripping the scrubs and wearing a shimmer and shine for tonight was a nice change. She wore the perfect emerald green sequined blouse with a pair of flowy palazzo pants to complement the suit and tie Garrison said he'd be wearing. She knew he'd look handsome. Butterflies still fluttered whenever she saw him.

Her aging mother had drawn Shirley back to her hometown of Charleston, South Carolina, but in the process of reestablishing her life, she'd found love. Or rather love had found her.

Shirley had been slow to accept Garrison's advances since they worked at the same place. It had everything to do with the well-known rule for dating—never mix business and pleasure. And, if she was being honest, a part of her was scared to open her heart to the potential of getting hurt. But with the gentle and not-so-gentle nudges from her friends and mother, not to mention Garrison's sweet Southern charm, she soon found herself in love.

"He's here," Shirley said, when the bright headlights from Garrison's truck shone through the front window.

"Your chariot awaits, ladies," Garrison said when they met him at the door. He cupped Mama's elbow and helped her down the porch steps, across the graveled driveway, and into the truck. He kept a step stool to make it easier for her to climb up into the cab. Next, he helped Shirley into the second row but not before tenderly kissing her on the hand.

"You look gorgeous," he said, in a low voice.

"Like mother, like daughter," Mama chimed out, making all of them chuckle. "I'm old, but I'm not deaf. At least not yet."

"Mama, what am I going to do with you?" Shirley asked, buckling her seat belt.

"You can't get rid of me, that's for sure. So love me."

"That I do, Mama, that I do."

Valet service welcomed them into the circular driveway when they arrived at the Christmas home.

"I'd hate to see the electricity bill for this place," Mama said as they admired the outdoor decor, which could only be described as a production. Lights not only blanketed the bushes but were wrapped around the enormous oak trees out front. Two colossal Nutcrackers flanked the wide porticos, and Christmas tunes piped merrily through unseen speakers.

"Between Mama's decorations and all of this tonight, I'd say I'm officially in the Christmas spirit," Shirley said.

Mama pulled her shawl tighter around her shoulders. "My decorations could never compare to this."

Shirley placed an arm on her mother's shoulder. "You're right. There's no comparison. Because as beautiful and extravagant as this all is, what you've done at our house holds all our family memories over the years. Even back to the Rudolph frame I made from popsicle sticks in third grade. That's what makes it special."

Mama reached up and patted Shirley's hand. "That's right, baby. So let's go in. I feel like shaking a tail feather."

"I'm not sure what kind of dancing you can do to 'Holly Jolly Christmas,' but let's go have fun."

Shirley stepped into the marble foyer and immediately spotted her closest friends from the hospital. Anne Mabry, Evelyn Perry, and Joy Atkins huddled together between a table of hors d'oeuvres and a table where two serving staff members were pouring mugs of apple cider. Since Shirley and her mother had eaten a hearty beef stew and rice dinner before getting dressed, she was only lured by the cinnamon scent of the apple cider.

Garrison helped her and her mother out of their coats and offered to take them to the coat check area.

"Can I catch back up with you in a few minutes?" he asked. "I see a benefactor I'd like to speak to before he gets swept away. Someone is always vying for his attention."

"Go ahead," Shirley insisted. She grabbed his hand and squeezed it. "I'm sure I'll be somewhere in this area."

"It won't be hard to find you. You're the prettiest woman here," he said, returning her squeeze.

Mama beamed. "I'm telling you. He's a keeper."

A table held brochures offering a self-guided tour of the home. Shirley had learned through the grapevine that the Christmas family hired a team of decorators to outfit each room. And they couldn't simply choose a theme to their own liking. Their decor had to connect to a story that was part of Charleston's history.

"I'll take one of these," Mama said, then went on her way.

"Shirley, you look absolutely radiant," Joy said as Shirley approached her friends with a cup of apple cider topped with whipped cream and a ribbon of caramel.

"I can say the same about you," Shirley said. "As a matter of fact, we all need to make sure we get a photo together by the Christmas tree."

"Which one?" Anne asked. "You haven't taken the tour yet, Shirl. There's one in every single room. Spectacular, I'm telling you. And I haven't pulled out a single ornament, ribbon, or garland at home. I'm still recovering from Thanksgiving."

"That makes two of us," Evelyn chimed in.

"Well, thanks to Mama, our house has been transformed. This afternoon she was even writing down some Christmas memories from my childhood in her journal."

"So she's still journaling?" Evelyn said. "That's great. Those are priceless treasures that you'll always have. I should follow in her footsteps."

"She does it whenever the mood strikes her, which is often," Shirley said, making ripples like a pebble thrown in a pond as she blew on her apple cider. "I've started doing it as well, but I'm not as consistent as she is."

Mama's fading memory had spurred her to begin to record parts of her life in journals before the memories slipped away. She'd filled three notebooks over the last year and had commented many times about how she hoped her journals would be a treasure to her family many years after she was gone. It also helped that she'd kept photo albums for most of her life, even being so organized as to have them in chronological order.

Shirley had amassed so many memories since she'd returned to Charleston and settled into her incredible nursing career at Mercy Hospital. She'd met amazing patients who had left an indelible mark on her heart. People like Mr. Benjamin Christmas. And then there were the mysteries at Mercy. She'd become a regular sleuth from the first month there.

"I tell you one thing. I'm excited to be here," Evelyn said. "The parties I attend with James at the university can be a tad bit stuffy. And quiet too. Even though the room is full, it's like not a creature is stirring."

"Not even a mouse," they all chimed in together.

Shirley finished her cider and placed her empty cup on a tray with others. In a matter of seconds, someone came to sweep it up. "Well, this party is anything but quiet," Shirley said. In addition to the self-guided tours, the delectable spread of foods for every palate, and the string ensemble playing Christmas music, a group of carolers had gathered in front of the Fraser fir tree in the front foyer. Curls of white and silver ribbon and embellished ornaments adorned the tree. The stems were covered with fake snow that looked so real Shirley could swear she felt a chill in the air.

Jingle bells chimed and grew loud enough to quiet the crowd. Shirley moved in anticipation toward the sound, unsure of what was about to take place. People streamed from the upstairs rooms and lined up on the landing and down the winding staircase.

Shirley leaned close to Joy as they walked with the flow of the other attendees. "Those carolers must really be something."

"I was thinking the same thing," Joy said, tucking a piece of hair behind her ear. "One thing I miss about my Texas neighborhood is the community carolers that came around at Christmastime every week in December. I can't carry a tune in a bucket, but I loved listening to them."

"A Christmas carol makes everything better," Shirley whispered.

"Which reminds me," Joy said. "Are you joining the Mercy carolers this year?"

"I haven't decided yet. I want to have a peaceful December without all the hustle and bustle. A few quiet get-togethers and some hot chocolate with friends every now and then is more than enough for me."

"I'm with you." Joy nodded. "That sounds nice."

Evelyn and Anne squeezed through the crowd in time to join their friends as a man appeared from behind the Christmas tree wearing a forest-green velvet jacket with a black satin collar. He approached a podium that had been placed in front of the voluminous tree and was joined by an older gentleman wearing a jacket of the same design but in a deep cranberry hue.

Shirley recognized the man in the red jacket as Nicholas Christmas, the seventy-two-year-old son of Benjamin Christmas. Shirley had learned over time that Nicholas didn't share his father's over-the-top love of the holidays, but it seemed he'd done something special to honor his memory. Usually clean-shaven with only a mustache, Nicholas had grown in a full white beard like his father had worn for years during December.

The man in the green jacket tilted the microphone until he had it at a comfortable height.

"Greetings to our Charleston family, friends, and special guests. My name is Tatum Everett Jr., from Tatum and Associates Law Firm. My family has served the Christmas family for thirty-eight years. As you all know, tonight is a bittersweet moment for everyone here. This was the most wonderful time of the year to Mr. Christmas. He not only embodied the spirit of all the lights, festivities, and parties, but he sincerely adored and shared the true meaning of Christmas. He didn't hesitate to tell everyone he knew, 'The real meaning of Christmas is Christ.'"

Shirley nodded. As much as Mr. Christmas had shared his favorite memories of his holiday traditions, he'd equally marveled in the love of Jesus. He'd shared many times that he was simply a vessel to spread God's love.

Mr. Tatum continued. "Even though he's no longer here with us, Mr. Christmas didn't leave us lacking. If you were in his presence for even a short period of time you could not leave without being changed. He had a quirky sense of humor, which is blatantly evident by the jackets that he left behind for his son and me to wear." He laughed and pulled at the collar. "Definitely not the tailored black or blue suits I'm used to wearing."

Nicholas briefly stepped forward to the podium and added his two cents. "He could never convince me to wear this when he was alive. It was the least I could do. This is my first time in this suit jacket, and also my last."

His face blushed red when he laughed—his cheeks were like roses and his nose like a cherry.

Tatum returned to the microphone. "This is going to be a non-traditional and unexpected moment during the opening of the annual festival of Christmas trees, but Mr. Christmas asked that a part of his will be read tonight."

Gasps and murmurs rolled over the crowd.

"This is definitely unconventional," Evelyn said. She fingered the long string of pearls that hung around her neck.

"That was his way. Mr. Christmas was always full of surprises," Shirley said.

She noticed Garrison standing across the room with her mother by his side. Mama held on to the bend of his elbow, leaning on him for support. The chilly morning and evening temperatures sometimes caused her arthritis to flare up. Shirley was thinking of the ways she could help alleviate her mother's achy joints when Tatum began to read a personal letter from Mr. Christmas.

"'To my family, friends, and the Charleston community. You're used to seeing me in all my splendor on this glorious night, but believe me, if I'm not there with you it means I'm in a much better place. You have touched my life in more ways than you probably know, and I hope I've done the same. The city of Charleston helped to make me the businessman and philanthropist that I dreamed to be. Many of my favorite organizations will continue to reap the benefits of the monetary investments I've made throughout the years. Those places have already been contacted. Except for one.'"

Tatum flipped the page of the letter, then steadied his eyes on Shirley. "'Mercy Hospital.'"

"Shirley, I believe he's looking directly at you," Anne whispered behind a cupped hand.

"I was thinking the same thing."

She looked over and caught Garrison's expression. If Mercy Hospital was set to receive a substantial donation from the Christmas estate, then Garrison was already calculating how much could be done with it, since he was hospital administrator and the main eyes to the budget.

Tatum cleared his throat before he continued. "'The roots of Mercy Hospital run deep, and its long-standing history has withstood gale-force hurricane winds and destructive fires. What can never be taken away is the kindness of the physicians, staff, and employees who provided extraordinary care during my illness.'"

Evelyn started a round of applause, and everyone in the room quickly joined in.

Tatum waited for the clapping to end before he continued. "'In return for their dedication and as a result of my sincere gratitude, I have bequeathed twenty-five million dollars to Mercy Hospital to use as the administrators and board of directors see fit.'"

Gasps filled the room for the second time that night.

"It's our own Mercy Christmas miracle," Joy said.

"And an answer to many prayers," Anne added.

Tatum held his hand up to quiet the room before he returned to the letter.

"'One thing all of you will remember about me is that I love puzzles and adventures. In order to secure the donation to Mercy Hospital, a number of people throughout the city have been contacted to help me pull off what I hope will be an engaging adventure. In order for Mercy to receive the donation, an appointed person will have to complete a scavenger hunt with ten clues. This person will be directly assisted by three people and three people only. Even if others hear the clues, they can't offer any insight. And although it's somewhat of a team effort, each item and the subsequent clues can only be claimed by the appointed person.'"

"That could be fun and stressful all at the same time," Anne said. "It looks like I need to turn the focus of my prayers to whoever will be carrying the weight of this on their shoulders."

"That's for sure," Shirley agreed. "I wonder who it will be."

Nicholas Christmas returned to the podium. "And that appointed person—chosen thoughtfully by my father—is Shirley Bashore."

Chapter Two

IT WAS A MISTAKE. SHIRLEY was sure of it. Because she thought she'd heard her name. Was it Cheryl Gilmore? Shelly McClemore? Whoever it was had a name that sounded so similar to hers that it shot a tinge of anxiety up her spine.

Shirley looked around the room for the stunned person who would basically be responsible for ensuring that Mercy Hospital would receive twenty-five million dollars. But all eyes were on her. Her heart thudded inside her chest. Shirley felt a hand on each of her arms, and then someone began to pat her on the back. They slightly nudged her toward the front as if she'd won the grand prize in a raffle, but her feet felt like heavy magnets attached to a metal floor.

"But how? Why?"

"Shirley, you clearly left an amazing impression on Mr. Christmas," Evelyn said. Her eyes twinkled like stars at midnight.

In fact, everyone in the room seemed to be filled with exhilaration, except for Shirley. She was shocked. Thankfully, Garrison sensed her hesitation and found his way to her side. It felt like she had been frozen for an hour, when in reality it could only have been a matter of seconds.

Garrison grabbed her hands, an act that steadied her legs and allowed her to swallow the lump stuck in her throat. He walked her to the podium, where she took her place between Nicholas Christmas and Tatum Everett Jr.

Her plans to have a restful Christmas holiday had just been changed. But how could she say no? She couldn't. Shirley forced a smile, even though inside she was a ball of nerves.

Tatum produced a gold foil envelope.

"This envelope, Ms. Bashore, contains your first clue. Upon your arrival at the location where each clue leads you, you'll receive the next clue as well as a customized ornament that should be added to the community Christmas tree at Mercy Hospital."

Nicholas twined his hands behind his back and rocked on his heels. "And so you know, there are no shortcuts. No one at these locations knows the location of the next clue. As a matter of fact, I don't even know the locations. My father entrusted only one person with that information, and even they shall remain anonymous."

Tatum reopened his portfolio and proceeded to read the next portion of the letter from Mr. Christmas.

"'If I know Shirley—and I do—she's surely shocked. But she's well able to accomplish the task at hand. In fact, she's told me of all the mysteries and miracles that have happened around Mercy Hospital. I was thoroughly entertained by her stories and got to know her friends, Joy Atkins, Anne Mabry, and Evelyn Perry, through her eyes. They're quite a bunch, from what I've heard and from what I've found out about them. That's why it wouldn't be right if I sent Shirley on this adventure without them. They will be her three assistants. The Christmas elves, if you will.'"

Tatum paused and looked across the sea of faces. Shirley did the same, except she looked directly at her friends. Their expressions spoke volumes. They were in. Joy gave her a thumbs-up and nudged Evelyn, who did the same. Anne nodded. Anne's husband, Ralph, kissed her on the cheek. He was Mercy's chaplain, and although Shirley couldn't bring him into her circle, she'd be the first to ask for his prayers.

"Let me start off by saying that I'm both honored and anxious to be chosen for this task. Even after all the memorable times I spent with Mr. Christmas, I never saw this coming. Then again, he built a reputation of being a man of surprises."

The crowd around her nodded in agreement.

"I can assure you that me and my little elves"—Shirley winked at her friends—"will do everything within our power to bring this donation home to Mercy Hospital."

Garrison's applause thundered behind her.

Tatum shook her hand firmly then gave her the envelope containing the first clue.

"This clue is not to be opened until Monday morning," he explained. He held up a finger. "And one more thing that I failed to mention. This entire quest must be completed by sunset on Christmas Day."

Garrison bent down to whisper in her ear. "No pressure. I believe in you."

"And I hope you believe in Christmas miracles too," she whispered back. No pressure? Who was he kidding? There was a ton of pressure.

Shirley spent the rest of the evening accepting the congratulations of all the party attendees who were more thrilled about her quest than she was. She was admiring the Christmas tree in the room the brochure listed as *Dreaming of a White Christmas*. The tree was shrouded in glittery snowflakes and white crystalized ornaments.

"This has to be—" Shirley stopped when she realized that the person she turned toward wasn't Anne. Instead, she bumped into a group of identical triplets who were standing so close behind her that she stumbled. They wore matching red cardigans with a string of pearls. It was like looking at Mrs. Santa Claus. Times three.

"Oh, I'm sorry," Shirley said.

"We're the Harper sisters. We don't want to disturb your house tour, but we wanted to let you know we're here if you need a helping hand. Or three," the first woman said. She had a beauty mark over her lip, the only feature that distinguished her from her sisters.

"I know what they said, but we've been in Charleston for generations. We know the ins and outs of this city better than anyone else. Besides, how in the world would anyone find out?"

"I have a feeling Mr. Christmas placed eyes and ears all around us," Shirley said, trying to convince them. "With a donation like the one at stake, I'm not willing to take any chances."

The sister sandwiched in the middle crossed her arms in slight agitation. "You'd be better off with the three of us as your helpers."

"If you change your mind, you know where to find us," the third sister said.

Actually, Shirley didn't, and it was the least of her worries.

They shuffled away, walking so close that their swaying hips gently knocked into each other.

Anne appeared by her side. "It looks like you've become the star of this entire shindig."

"I wish they were more concerned about the stars on top of the Christmas trees than they are with me," Shirley said. She looked at the people who were openly following her every move, and those who tried to pretend like they weren't.

Anne wrapped her arms around Shirley's waist. She was wearing the new hand lotion Shirley had given all of them last week. She smelled like warm cinnamon cookies. "I can't imagine how overwhelmed you're feeling. But remember, you've got a pretty good bunch of supersleuths by your side. It's going to be fun."

"I certainly hope so."

"Don't think about the money."

"How can I *not* think about the money? It would be one of the largest donations in the history of the hospital. I caught the wishful look in Garrison's eyes too."

"There's certainly a look in his eyes, but it's not about the money. It's about you. I've seen that look in Ralph's eyes for the last forty years. I'd know it anywhere. It's love. And I think I'm starting to see that same spark in Joy's eyes too." She gestured across the room. "Roger just arrived."

Roger Gaylord was one of Mercy Hospital's benefactors and belonged to one of Charleston's most upstanding families. He was also courting Joy—or at least trying.

Joy hadn't been sure she'd be ready to date when Roger began to show interest. Although she'd refused to call it a date at the time, she'd enjoyed their first outing together to Mercy's Christmas fundraiser last year. Since then, their friendship had grown at a slow and steady pace, just like she said she preferred. Shirley had seen Roger drop by the gift shop on occasion. They had an easy way with each other. Roger didn't push, and Shirley knew Joy appreciated that.

From the time Shirley had met Joy, her friend had spoken fondly of her late husband, Wilson. They'd married right out of college. It would take time for her to get comfortable seeing other people. Even though Roger and his Charleston-born-and-raised family held a high place in the community, he was an unpretentious man. Joy had told Shirley before that she wasn't impressed by his great wealth—she was impressed by his great heart. It was evident by the smile on her face that she was enjoying his presence tonight.

Garrison walked into the room. Her mother was by his side, again using his arm to steady her gait.

"I think Mama has done enough walking for tonight," Shirley said as she noticed a slight grimace on her mother's face. She knew Mama wouldn't complain and request to leave so Shirley would bow out early for her sake.

"We've been looking for you," Garrison said.

"You two and everyone else," Shirley answered.

"Does that mean you're ready to call it a night?" Garrison suggested.

"That's probably not a bad idea," Shirley said, suddenly finding herself about to stifle a yawn. "Unless you think I shouldn't. I'd hate to seem rude."

"If they knew you like I did, they'd know it was already past your bedtime anyway," Garrison added with a slight chuckle.

He'd learned very early in their dating relationship that he shouldn't waste his money on late-night movies because the dark theater basically beckoned her to lean her head on his shoulder and doze off for the duration of the movie. Every now and then he was able to squeeze time enough for nightcap at a coffee shop after dinner, but that was it. Shirley preferred the early-morning hospital shifts for good reason.

"If you're leaving now, then Ralph and I will walk out with you," Anne said. "Let me send him to the coat check, and we'll meet you out front at the valet."

"That's a plan," Garrison said. "I'll grab Ralph for you since I need to head to the coat check too."

Shirley was surprised at the size of the crowd when she descended the steps from the tour she'd been taking on the second floor. Thankfully many of the people hadn't yet arrived when the grand announcement was made, but word would definitely get around. She noticed a couple of folks pointing in her direction. Although she'd already been enjoying herself for two hours, it seemed as if the party was just starting. Some guests were just beginning to arrive, and the food was still plentiful.

"It looks like it could last all night," Shirley said to Anne, taking in all the festivities like she was seeing them for the first time.

Garrison returned and draped her pashmina around her shoulders.

"Do you have the envelope?" he asked her. He said it casually, as if he were asking if she had a spare tissue, but she was possibly carrying a piece of Mercy's history in her gold clutch. She'd brought one just large enough for keys, compact, and a lipstick, all of which didn't compare in value to what this first clue and each of the others could bring.

Shirley patted her clutch. "Safe and secure. And not to be opened until Monday morning."

Anne slid her arm into the sleeve of the coat Ralph offered. "And Joy, Evelyn, and I will be right by your side."

"How early can you get there?"

The scent of freshly brewed coffee welcomed Shirley into the gift shop at six o'clock Monday morning, earlier than usual. Joy's famous brew wasn't set to start until six forty-five, but this morning they needed the extra time *and* the extra caffeine. The sun had yet to take its place for the day, but the ladies were bright-eyed and ready.

Once they were all settled at the table in the back of the gift shop with their coffee, Shirley withdrew the envelope. She slid her finger under the sealed tab and pulled out the note inside, reading it to herself before sharing it aloud.

"'It's the perfect season for the holiday treat. Dark chocolate and whipped cream, oh so sweet. It wraps you in a hug like a lifelong best friend. Make haste, run along, and sip till the end.'"

Joy threw her hands up. "Shirley, here we all were worried about these clues and this one is super easy. This is going to be a cinch."

Shirley blew out a soft breath. "So where is this clue taking us?"

"To Two Buddies Coffee Shop," Joy said without a second thought.

Evelyn nodded. "That makes sense. I haven't been there in a while, but they're always known for their seasonal peppermint hot chocolate at this time of year. And the clue said lifelong best friends. And that means they're—"

"Two buddies," Shirley said. "You're right. We were worried for nothing. One clue down and only nine more to go. We'll be done well before Christmas Day. So, who would like to go out for hot chocolate this evening?"

"I'd love to," Evelyn said. "They have a delicious Reuben sandwich there too, come to think of it."

Anne dumped a caramel-flavored creamer into her mug and swirled it with a wooden stirrer. "I'll have to pass, ladies. Ralph and I are hosting a Bible study at our house tonight. This has given me an idea though. I have everything I need at home to put together a hot cocoa bar. I think I'll arrange a treat box and drop it off to Lili and Addie. They'll love that, and I'll get a chance to spend some time with my granddaughter. Sometimes I miss the sound of her little feet running through the house."

Shirley slid the clue back into the envelope and tucked it in the side of her tote bag. "What about you, Joy?"

"I'll have to pass as well," Joy said. "It's time for my trim at the salon."

"Then it's the two of us," Shirley said to Evelyn.

"Are you sure Garrison won't mind if I steal you away for the evening?"

"Trust me. He's trying his best not to add any pressure to this whole thing, but I know he wants this donation for Mercy probably more than anyone else. He wouldn't dare do anything to mess things up. Like I told the Harper sisters, Mr. Christmas probably has eyes and ears all around the city."

"Then it will be good to catch up with you, my friend," Evelyn said. "It's been a while since we've had a heart-to-heart."

"Now you girls are making me jealous," Anne said. "Would it be bad if I ditched the Bible study tonight?"

The ladies settled into familiar laughter and conversation as the sun rose. They were about to pack up and go their separate ways when they heard someone knocking on the glass of the locked gift shop door.

"The aroma of the coffee is luring visitors already," Shirley said, commenting on the specially ordered coffee from Houston that had become a favorite of staff and guests.

"I bet it's Dr. Barnhardt, Dr. Lyle, or Rose from the birthing center," Evelyn said.

Joy stood and peeked around the corner. "Wrong, wrong, and wrong. It's Aurora."

"We all know Aurora," Shirley said as Joy scurried to open the door. "She doesn't visit without a reason."

Aurora Kingston blew into the room like a gale wind. "Ah, the people I wanted to see and all in the same place. How lucky am I?"

"Good morning, Aurora," they all chimed together.

Aurora paused for a moment to tap out a text message. When she finished, she looked up at them with pleading in her eyes. "I missed you all at the Christmas mansion. I arrived later than I meant to, but I'd barely had time to drink my apple cider when I heard the news." She looked at Shirley. "It's quite a feat, but I'm sure you're up to the task."

"I pray so," Shirley said.

"And not to put anything else on your plates, but…" She clasped her hands and squeezed her eyes tight. "Can you ladies head the committee for Mercy's Festival of Christmas Trees? Please? Pretty please with sugar on top?" she asked, running her words together so fast they sounded like one sentence.

Aurora continued like she didn't want to give them the chance to decline. "The Mercy on the Harbor exhibit, our new Mercy museum. It makes sense. You all are naturals at bringing things together, and with you I know it will be a success." She stopped and raised her hand. "Now I know you all may think this is another one of my bright ideas. And it is."

No one spoke, but that didn't deter Aurora from presenting the request.

Aurora walked over to the coffeepot and poured the brew into her insulated mug while she chatted away. "You know how full my plate is around this time of year. Honestly, it's not only full, it's over-flowing. I have the highest confidence that you ladies can pull this off." Aurora studied them with bright eyes.

"Well, I guess we could—" Evelyn started.

"Thank you, thank you, thank you," Aurora said. "I can imagine it now. A forest of live fir, spruce, and pine right in our own lobby that won't compare to anything else in the entire city." She slid a piece of paper from her leather portfolio. "Of course, I've already compiled a list of the organizations and businesses that may want to participate. I've also drafted some guidelines to get you started." She shoved the pages into Evelyn's hands.

"Thanks for the coffee," she said, and then she blew out as quickly as she'd blown in.

"I was going to say that I guess we could think about it," Evelyn said slowly.

"You can't help that your lips don't move as fast at Aurora's," Shirley said with a chuckle.

"Maybe we should be honored that she asked us," Anne said. "My mother used to always remind me that your reputation precedes you. I'd say we have a reputation of getting things done around the halls of Mercy Hospital."

Shirley stretched her arm out so that her hand was on the middle of the table. Anne, Evelyn, and Joy each placed a hand on top of hers—a sign of friendship and unity.

"We're all in this together," Shirley said.

Tiny wrinkles formed at the corner of Joy's eyes when she smiled. "Always have been, always will be."

That day Shirley worked tirelessly in the labor and delivery unit. She skipped lunch and instead opted for a quick snack of trail mix and an iced green tea when she had a moment to steal away to the break room. All of her thoughts of maintaining a healthy eating plan as much as she could during the holidays disappeared when she spotted half a box of doughnuts, shiny with glaze.

"Blame it on Santa," she said to herself, and scooped one up with a napkin. She told herself she wouldn't dare touch the fudge and walnut brownies sprinkled with powdered sugar.

Faye, a fellow nurse, walked in. "You blame it on Santa, I blame it on the patient families that keep bringing goodies to the nurses' station. How do they expect me to keep my dainty figure?" Faye bumped her full hip against Shirley's. "So it's about time you start your wild goose chase throughout Charleston. It's all everyone is talking about."

Shirley hoped she wouldn't have to recount the night again. She'd done it at least four times already with her well-meaning coworkers who were excited about the prospect of having some of their patient programs funded and groundbreaking technology and medical equipment actualized.

Faye lowered her voice. "What's the first clue? Come on. I won't say a word. I promise." Faye pointed a finger to herself then to Shirley. "It's me and you."

"I'm going to choose not to do that, Faye," Shirley said. "We all know you're a problem solver around here, and if you happened to slip and help me with this clue, my conscience couldn't handle it."

That wasn't the only reason. Shirley knew that Faye couldn't keep a secret to save her life. The entire hospital staff would know by the end of the shift.

"I tell you," Faye said, bringing her voice up to normal levels. "Mr. Christmas chose the right one for sure. I wish you all the luck."

Shirley dropped her napkin in the trash. "Luck won't get me as far as prayer, that's for sure."

"Do you know why you were chosen of all people?" Faye asked.

"I can't say for certain, but looking back in hindsight, I think he gave me a hint that something was coming."

Shirley put the cream soda and the small vase of hydrangeas for Mr. Christmas on the table nearest his bed. She propped her hands on her hips and looked at the two wardrobe racks of suits and dress shirts, all in various shades of blue, gray, and brown. There was even an all-white ensemble.

"Wow! What's the special occasion?"

Mr. Christmas handed a blue and red paisley tie to a man standing nearby. He was a tailor, and probably Mr. Christmas's personal one. Shirley could tell by the measuring tape that hung over his shoulders and the pin cushion strapped around his wrist.

"Shirley, what do you think of this tie with the navy blue suit?"

"I'm partial to navy blue," Shirley said. "It's one of my favorite colors. And I like this one." She ran her hand down the arm of an ocean-blue suit. "It reminds me of the beach."

"That's one of my top options as well," Mr. Christmas said. He pointed at the suit and the tailor pulled it from the rack. "Please have it monogrammed on the inside as you've always done. Nothing about that has changed."

Shirley popped open the tab of the can of cream soda and poured a taste into a cup. When he'd mentioned that he'd randomly thought about how he used to love cream soda, Shirley was happy to oblige his taste buds. Cream soda was one of her favorites as well.

"You never told me what you're getting all dressed up for," Shirley said, watching as Mr. Christmas took a taste of his soda then held the cup out for another pour.

Mr. Christmas finished his drink and set the empty cup beside him with a satisfied smile. "I'm getting prepared to go home. I'm not sure when it will be, but everyone who knows me knows that I like to be prepared."

Shirley frowned. Mr. Christmas was certainly wealthy enough to have a private nurse and any hospital equipment he needed transferred to the comfort of his home. She was so used to coming to his private suite at the end of her shifts to spend time with him though. She would miss that.

"Have you gotten word about when you'll be discharged?" she asked.

Mr. Christmas chuckled. "That's not the home I meant. I mean my eternal home with the Father. God has blessed me with an abundant life, and when He calls me I want to be ready."

A lump caught in Shirley's throat. She was at a loss for words, and that was something that didn't happen often.

"In case you haven't noticed, I like to be in control. I wanted to do it this way, otherwise my son may have me dressed in a clown's suit." He belted a deep laugh that made him cough. He scribbled his signature across a page the tailor gave them, and then the tailor covered over the wardrobe racks and left quickly and quietly.

Shirley rolled Mr. Christmas over to the windows to the amazing view the room offered. At this time of year, Charleston Harbor was dotted with boats in the distance. The waves rolled in and crashed across the shoreline, where children built sandcastles, the young sunbathed, and seagulls dove from the skies to the waters.

"Come. Take a seat with me," Mr. Christmas said.

Shirley did as the old man she'd come to admire—even love—requested. Her legs were feeling weak from his recent words. "I'm getting prepared to go home." She knew it was a possibility, but the reality of it weighed her down.

"I don't remember the last time I felt sand between my toes," Mr. Christmas said. "I wish I would've done more of that."

"It seems to me that you're a fun person based on your fabulous Christmas parties that everyone talks about."

"That's because I worked my fingers to the bone all year, and that was usually the only time I slowed down to enjoy the fruits of my labor. Besides, with a last name like mine it's basically a requirement. Have you ever been to one of my parties, Shirley? I hate to admit it, but I rarely know everyone on the guest list."

"I haven't had the pleasure," Shirley said.

"You'll be invited to the next one," Mr. Christmas said. "You can be sure of it."

"I would like that," Shirley said, watching as her elderly friend's eyes begin to get heavy with sleep.

"I want everyone to remember me at Christmastime this year. I'm not sure I'll make it."

"Only God knows," Shirley said.

Mr. Christmas was a man of faith and had never been shy about openly discussing death, because he knew he'd accepted eternal life.

"You can help them remember me, Shirley. I know you can do it."

"They'll never forget you because of the way you've lived your life," she told him. "Love above all."

"Yes," Mr. Christmas said before slipping off into sleep. "I know you can do it."

He dozed off with a smile on his face.

By the time she met up with Evelyn at Two Buddies Coffee Shop, Shirley couldn't believe the number of people who had approached her asking for a hint about the clue or offering to help. Honesty had always run through Shirley's blood. She'd never cheated on a test, always returned money to the cashier when she received too much change. She wasn't about to act differently now.

The teenaged barista handed Shirley an oversized ceramic mug shaped like Rudolph. A red bulb nose protruded from the side. She'd ordered the *Leader of the Sleigh* and quickly realized it wasn't simply a hot cocoa. It was an entire dessert. A mountain of thick whipped cream sat on top and was sprinkled with chocolate chips and red and white confetti sugar crystals. Four peppermint sticks stuck out from the cup.

Shirley put it on the table across from Evelyn's snowman concoction and turned it around.

"I don't even know where to start," Shirley said once the barista brought them two long-handled spoons.

"Let's dig in. We're going to scoop our way from the top to the bottom." Evelyn shed her coat and hung it on the back of the chair.

"This year we added a fudge brownie to the bottom," the barista proudly announced as she dropped a stack of napkins on the table. "Enjoy. And the manager will be back any moment now. I'm sorry I don't know about the ornament and the…" She paused and shrugged. "Did you say a clue?"

"Don't worry about that at all," Evelyn said. She swiped her bangs across her face. "Sometimes when you get old, you get things mixed up. We'll wait for the manager."

"Okay, sure," the barista said.

"Who are you calling old?" Shirley teased. "Speak for yourself."

"I'm not old either," Evelyn said. "I prefer to call it seasoned."

"Speaking of being seasoned in a cooking sort of way. I emailed you Mama's recipe for her okra soup earlier today. I tried to gauge the measurements for all the ingredients when we made it a couple of weeks ago, but she's been cooking it so long it's second nature.

A handful of this, a pinch of that. I only learned by watching her with a hawk's eye."

"I told James I'd try my best," Evelyn said.

Shirley heard the sudden screech of tires, and her body flinched at the imminent crash, even though they were seated safely inside, far from the doors and wall of windows. The sound of metal meeting metal interrupted the Christmas music playing in the corner coffee shop. There were loud scrapes across the wooden floor as people bolted from their seats, and within a blink, the high-beam glare of two headlights brightened the shop as the car came to a stop.

"Oh my," Evelyn said, clutching her scarf.

Instinctively, Shirley rushed outside to see if she needed to offer any medical assistance. Both drivers, however, had exited their vehicles to survey the damage. One of the cars had jumped the curb and stopped inches short of hitting a lamppost wrapped in green pine garland and a red bow. A man, who looked to Shirley to be in his midfifties, gripped the side of his head as he surveyed his car. Deployed air bag. Crushed front bumper. Busted headlight. The side view mirror on the driver's side dangled from two wires.

"Did anyone call 911?" Shirley heard someone ask.

"I'm on it," a different voice answered.

Shirley approached the first man cautiously but with care. "Sir, can I offer you any assistance?" He was clothed in jeans and a heavy sweater, so she didn't see physical cuts on his extremities or body, but there were minor abrasions on his face, most likely caused by the air bag. *After the adrenaline wears off, he'll feel it,* Shirley thought.

"That nut ran the red light," he said, pointing to the other car stalled in the middle of the intersection. "I can't believe it."

Shirley let him rant and blow off steam. It was the last thing anyone would want to deal with during the Christmas season, or any other time of year for that matter, but at least everyone seemed to have escaped with only minor injuries. Evelyn appeared by Shirley's side with a bottle of water, which she promptly opened and handed to the frazzled man.

"I need to sit down," he finally said.

Shirley watched him stumble slightly, and in three quick steps she was by his side. She helped guide him to a safe space on the sidewalk. "You should probably take it easy for a moment."

"Thank you so much. Nerves, most likely. You know how they say your life flashes before your eyes? I didn't even have time for that to happen. Didn't even see it coming."

The teen barista who had helped Shirley and Evelyn earlier pushed through the crowd that had gathered.

"Mr. Marlon, are you all right? Oh man. I didn't realize that was you."

"I'm fine," he assured her. "But can you look on the front seat and see if my brownies survived?" He waved his hand in the air like he was trying to gather his thoughts. "And there should be a box from the print shop with the new coupons for the Hot Cocoa Run. Make sure these fine women get a few for coming to check on me."

"Sure thing," she said, skittering to the car. She pulled out two brown shopping bags, then pushed the door closed with her foot. "That's my manager, by the way," she said to Shirley as she passed by.

Mr. Marlon looked up to her with questioning eyes. "Somebody looking for me?"

"If they are, they can wait," Shirley assured him. "I'm Shirley." There was no way she could ask him about a clue or an ornament. Nothing. Now wasn't the time.

Shirley heard the growing whir of ambulance and police sirens as the first responders arrived. She waited with a watchful eye until the paramedics ushered both drivers to the ambulance to be checked for injuries.

She and Evelyn returned to their table in the back of the coffee shop, their hot cocoa now cold. The teenage barista graciously offered them a replacement.

Evelyn sighed. "I wasn't expecting this kind of excitement tonight. How unfortunate. In more ways than one."

"I don't think we should bother the manager about a clue today," Shirley said. "He's got bigger things to think about. I guess we'll have to come back tomorrow."

After settling everything with the police officer and the offending driver, Marlon stood at the door and watched as a tow truck hitched his damaged vehicle and lifted it to the back of the trailer. As soon as he stepped into the coffee shop, the barista pulled him to the side and pointed in Shirley and Evelyn's direction.

"What's this about a clue or an ornament that you're looking for here that I'm supposed to have?" Marlon asked.

Shirley gave him the abridged version of the announcement that had taken place two days ago. "I really didn't want to bother you about it, considering what just happened."

"Man," Marlon said, disappointment in his voice. "I wish I did have a clue or one of those ornaments. Maybe then I'd also have a cut of that cash. I might need it for my vehicle damage. The guy who hit me didn't even have insurance." He shook his head. "But there's no clue here."

"You know nothing about it?" Shirley asked.

Marlon shook his head. "Nothing but what you told me."

Shirley was at a loss. "Thank you for your time, and also the coupons. I'll be back for sure, and I'll share these coupons with my friends and send them here as well. In the meantime, I hope everything works out for you."

"Same to you," Marlon said. "Most of the time the thing you're looking for is right under your nose."

Chapter Three

MERCY HOSPITAL WAS IN A prime location to allow for lunchtime strolls to quaint and tasty eateries, boutique clothing stores, novelty shops, and the like. Fortunately, the temperatures were still comfortable enough for Shirley to steal away for an early lunch with Joy and Anne. Afterward they visited a craft shop that had just had its grand opening the month before.

"He knew absolutely nothing about it," Shirley said to Joy. She ran her hand across a rust-colored chenille throw with fringed edges. She hadn't intended on purchasing any Christmas gifts on this brief outing, but her mother would love it. She enjoyed tucking throws around her lap at home and carried one with her whenever she left the house—to church, to Dot's house, and on the days she went to the senior citizen center.

"I was sure I was right," Joy said. She bit the corner of her lip. "At least it made sense to me. I hate that I sent you on a wild goose chase."

"It wasn't that at all," Shirley assured her. "We should expect to be stumped a bit by good old Mr. Christmas. We have to figure out what's next."

"But until then we have plenty of things to think about for the Christmas tree festival."

"You've got that right," Shirley said. The communications and technology departments had moved swiftly to update information about Mercy's Festival of Christmas Trees to the hospital's website with the information from Aurora, and they'd already received sixty-three applications of interest. The problem was, there were only twenty-five slots available. Any more than that and it *would* be like walking into a forest.

Shirley peeked into the wicker shopping basket hooked over Anne's arm. There were bundles of soft pink, baby blue, and canary yellow yarn that her friend planned to use to knit hats for the preemies in the NICU. "Did you find everything you were looking for?"

"The best organic yarn they make," Anne said. "I've been inspired by the prayer quilts you started making again with your mom. I only intended to knit hats for the holidays, but I'd bet you two elf shoes that I'll keep going. I've collected quite a stash of yarns for hats, booties, and blankets."

"You ladies are crafty," Joy complimented.

"Maybe. But no one else has your green thumb. I can't even keep a fake plant alive." Shirley laughed.

Joy headed toward the back of the shop. "I'm going to check out the community bulletin board while you two pay for your purchases. I wouldn't mind taking some classes when the new year begins."

Shirley pushed her debit card into the card reader to pay for the first of three gifts she planned to buy her mother.

The woman behind the counter told Shirley of all the neighborhood tours she hoped to take to view Christmas lights. "My father used to pack the entire family in the station wagon and drive through the neighborhoods at least once a week during the holidays," she said.

"My parents did same thing, except it was only two of us in the back. I can't imagine six children stuffed in the car."

"We were like a can of sardines, but we loved every minute of it," the woman said, folding the throw in a neat triangle. She wrapped it in gold tissue paper and nestled it tightly in a gift box.

"Hopefully, you'll get the opportunity to visit Mercy's Festival of Christmas Trees too. My invitation is premature, but it should be open for visitors by the end of next week until the New Year."

"I hope I can do more than visit. I submitted my interest application this morning as soon as I saw it online. Well, actually my niece told me about it. She works at Mercy and knows I've been knitting ornaments all year. Now I know exactly what I'm going to do with them." She handed Shirley a receipt. "Lyla, a daughter of one of my closest friends, recently opened Poppy's Sweet Shoppe. She had this great idea for a Christmas tree full of gigantic peppermints, candy canes, and marshmallows. She came by and helped me with the application since she was completing hers too. All this technology can be confusing for us older folks."

"That was sweet of her. Pun intended," Shirley said.

"When will we know if we've been chosen? I'm sure we were some of the first businesses to apply."

"You should hear something soon," Shirley said.

They'd already asked Aurora to close the application window and briefly discussed the best way to choose the participants. Shirley was pretty sure they'd settled on a random lottery process as the easiest and fairest method.

"Thank you and have a great day," Shirley said. "Maybe I'll see you during the Christmas tree festival."

"Anne, Shirley, come and see this." Joy called from a nook in the back of the store.

"I bet she found the saltwater taffy," Anne said. "No one can resist it once they taste the samples."

"That's the last thing my teeth need," Shirley said. "I had a cavity at my last dental exam. Do you know how long it's been since I've had a cavity?"

Joy stood in front of the community bulletin board, tapping on one of the flyers. "We may have something here. You know that coupon you gave me from Two Buddies? It has this same logo on it for the 5K Hot Cocoa Run. I'm sure of it."

Shirley stepped closer to examine the colorful flyer. The majority of the text was transposed on top of an oversized graphic of a red mug of hot cocoa with frothy whipped cream. It advertised a 5K run happening the next Saturday. Her mouth dropped open. She pulled out her phone and snapped a photo of the flyer. "You're right. It's worth a try. It definitely fits the clue."

"There's one problem, though," Anne said. "The registration deadline has passed."

"I'm calling anyway. What do we have to lose?"

They hurried back to Mercy and headed straight to the records department, where they found Evelyn organizing files in the Vault. The area had come a long way since Evelyn had finally gotten her hands on it. It had gone from damp, dusty, and crowded to airy, organized, and dust bunny free.

Evelyn closed the door enough for privacy but left it open enough that she could see anyone who walked into the department. "Perfect timing. Everyone's still out to lunch."

Shirley dialed the number on the flyer then put the call on speaker phone.

"Hello, yes," she said, when the voice on the other end answered. "I'm calling about the 5K Hot Cocoa Run that's happening this Saturday."

"Unfortunately, the deadline was last week, so you're late. And because this is a popular run, we don't have any spaces available. We're filled to the max."

Shirley couldn't imagine that Mr. Christmas would send them to an event that they couldn't get access to. She looked at her friends. Their gazes urged her to continue.

"I realize the deadline has passed, but I was hoping you could *clue* me in to how I could still participate."

The woman paused. "Did you say clue?"

"I did," Shirley said. "I know this may sound crazy, but would you know anything about a clue and an ornament?"

"Ma'am, what's your name?"

"Shirley Bashore from Mercy Hospital."

"Hold on, please," she said, without waiting for a response. The phone fell silent.

"I think this is it," Shirley said. Her heart fluttered in excitement.

"The office for the running club that's hosting the event is about ten minutes away from here," Joy said. "You can probably run by on the way home. I mean, if this is the answer to the first clue." She crossed her fingers on both hands and put them under her chin.

"Are you still here?" the woman asked as soon as she returned.

"Yes," Shirley said.

"Ms. Bashore, you have two race bibs reserved for your name—one for you and one for another runner."

"Race bib? Runner?"

"Yes, Ms. Bashore. In order to receive the package waiting here for you, you have to complete the 5K run."

Shirley wasn't sure what to say. That was the last thing she expected. She'd adopted a healthier lifestyle over the past few months and enjoyed leisurely strolls through the neighborhood with Garrison or her mother, but she'd never been very athletic. Ever. This was all going downhill fast.

"I've never run a 5K before. How far is that? Over three miles, right?"

"Yes ma'am. And no worries. You don't have to actually run the entire thing. You can walk if you'd like. You just need to cross the finish line."

"And you said I have two race bibs?"

"Yes. The instructions here say there are no stipulations on who your running—or walking—partner can be. Anyone you like."

Shirley almost laughed aloud at the look of relief that seemed to wash over her friends' faces. They would undoubtedly help her if she asked, but they would also graciously bow out if they could.

The woman shared that Shirley could pick up the race registrations from the office that evening or arrive early Saturday morning before the race.

"I know who'll gladly run by my side. At least I hope he will."

"Garrison?" Evelyn replied. "Oh, he'd be crazy not to. He'll do it for sure."

By the end of the day, Shirley found out that Evelyn was right.

"Of course I will," Garrison said as he walked Shirley to her car. "Especially if it gets us one step closer to that donation."

"One step closer but nine more to go," Shirley said. "How could Mr. Christmas have known that I'd figure out the clue in time? When I thought about it, I remembered seeing a flyer posted at the coffee shop when we walked in. I didn't pay much attention to it. That guy Marlon said that what I was looking for would be right under my nose. But what if Joy had never seen the flyer on the bulletin board?"

"First of all, Mr. Christmas was a very intelligent man, and he chose you with success in mind. Even with that, I'm not sure what would've happened if you'd never solved the first clue, but that doesn't matter. Because you did." He took the items Shirley was carrying and placed them carefully on the back seat, then opened the driver's door for her.

"My concern is for you. Do you think you can do this? You look tired."

Shirley definitely could have used some extra rest, but she didn't think she looked like it. She flipped down the visor mirror to check for under-eye circles.

"Yes, you must be tired," he said, touching her cheek softly. "Because you've been running through my mind all night."

"Oh, you," Shirley said. She playfully slapped his hand away and flipped the visor back up. "I thought you were being serious."

"I am serious about the fact that you've been on my mind," Garrison said. He loosened his necktie—the dark blue one with light blue vertical stripes that she'd bought him for his birthday. "I don't want you to stress too much about this donation."

"You said yourself that it will be the largest one in Mercy history. I think stress comes with the mission, unfortunately." She blew out a breath. "I keep telling myself that this is supposed to be fun. That's what Mr. Christmas would want me to feel. And he definitely didn't want Mercy Hospital to miss out on the gift. He loved us just as much as we loved him."

"I agree," Garrison said.

Shirley's cell phone buzzed in the pocket of her scrubs. "Excuse me for a second," she said, reading the notification on her screen.

"One hundred fifty-seven. Anne texted that we have one hundred fifty-seven applicants for twenty-five slots for Mercy's Festival of Christmas Trees. There are going to be a whole lot of disappointed people around the city."

Shirley drummed the steering wheel and looked up at Garrison. His wheels were turning. She could tell by the way he bit his bottom lip.

"How many more trees can we fit in the atrium?"

"Five. Maybe ten more before it starts looking too crowded. But ten is definitely the max to stay within the guidelines the fire department gave us. Safety first."

Her words made Garrison pause. "If the fire marshal has given us permission to have thirty-five trees, then let's have thirty-five trees. It doesn't fix the problem, but at least it will make ten more people happy."

Shirley sent out a group text with Garrison's request, and the messages began to ding repeatedly to her phone. She read them all before updating Garrison.

"We'll make a call to the Christmas tree farm in the morning and ask them to reserve ten more trees for us. By the end of the day tomorrow we'll make the random selections and notify the organizations and businesses that are chosen, as long as they fall within our guidelines and stipulations."

The committee's random selection dry test had pulled out a few questionable choices, and after reviewing the applications, Evelyn had made the executive decision to eliminate them.

"Sounds easy enough," Garrison said, looking pleased. He checked his watch. "I need to get back and finish preparing for my meeting. I'll be working late, but hopefully I can swing by later this evening."

"I'm looking forward to it," Shirley said. "But if I don't answer it's because I'm buried under Christmas decorations. Since the party at the Christmas mansion, Mama has taken her decorating to another level. Let me tell you. The woman is out of control. And maybe it's a mistake, but I'm letting her do whatever she wants."

"She's lived life a long time. She deserves it. Let her enjoy herself."

Shirley had come to appreciate her mother in her later years. They had bumped heads from time to time when Shirley moved back to Charleston from Atlanta. She wanted to be the dutiful caregiving daughter, but her mother felt she was trying to steal her independence. They'd come to a healthy place when they realized they needed each other in their own way—not only as mother and daughter but as friends. Regardless of her age, Shirley now understood that she would always be her mama's baby girl.

When Shirley pulled into the driveway beside Dot's car, she noticed the open windows right away. That could only mean one thing. Mama had been cooking. Getting her mother to stop fixing meals unattended was like pulling teeth.

Shirley had even started meal prepping over the weekends so her mother would have healthy food at hand, and it also eased Shirley's concerns when she was away at work. But that didn't stop her mother from dabbling in the kitchen whenever she had the urge.

And evidently, she'd had the urge.

Christmas music and the voices of her mother and her lifelong friend, Dot, spilled from the open windows. Her mother and Dot had made memories together as married women and continued their special bond now as widows. It was Dot who had called Shirley and expressed her concern about her friend's sometimes fading memories and absentmindedness.

"Before you say a word, I only slightly burned some sugar cookies. I didn't smoke up the entire house."

"We dumped the first batch and tried something else," Dot said. She pulled Shirley into a hug, enveloping her in her soft scent of floral lotion.

"Gingersnaps," her mother announced. Her face lit up. "Do you remember how much you used to love them? I'll never forget the time I thought your dad was eating them, but you were taking two every night and hiding them in your pillowcase." She tapped her chin and looked around the room. "I'll have to write that down."

Shirley dropped her lunch bag on the kitchen table. "I have good news. We found the location of the first clue."

"Oh good," her mother said, untying her apron and hanging it on a hook by the pantry door.

"What was the ornament?" Dot asked. Mama had already filled her friend in on every detail from that night.

Shirley plopped down on the sofa then kicked off her shoes. "I actually don't have the ornament or the next clue yet. I have to complete the 5K Hot Cocoa Run first."

"Well, have mercy. How are you going to do that?" her mother asked. "Please don't tell me you have to come in first place too."

"Thanks for the vote of confidence, Mama." She laughed. "But I don't have to actually run. I can walk, and Garrison is going to walk with me. And no, we don't have to cross the finish line first, we just have to cross it."

"That's a relief," Dot said.

"I think Garrison walking with you may be against the rules. They specifically said you could only have three people help you, and you already have your Mercy crew together."

Mama had retired from Mercy Hospital after twenty-four years. She loved patient care as much as Shirley and had built the same kind of lasting relationships. Over the years she'd been recognized for her distinguished service and significant contributions to the hospital. She was loved by patients and staff alike, and the feeling was mutual. Her mother wanted to see the donation check written to Mercy Hospital as much as everyone else.

"Don't worry, Mama. I had them reread the stipulations several times to make sure Garrison could walk with me, and they assured me it was correct."

"Then if you're with Garrison, you're in good hands," her mother stated.

The way Mama adored Garrison let Shirley know he was a good man. A very good man. Her mother often compared his character and some of his tendencies to Shirley's father, Charles. Shirley had always prayed that the man in her future would align with the way her father lived his life, loved his wife, and loved his children. He also had the same kind of drive as her father, and when Garrison knew there was something Shirley needed to tackle, he pushed her to pursue it—sometimes gently and sometimes not.

"I can't exactly train for a 5K three days before it happens," Shirley said. "I admit that I'm not at the peak of physical fitness, but my goal isn't to win, it's to finish."

Garrison lifted his hands in surrender. When he'd come to visit yesterday, she'd assumed it was so they could spend quality time together. Her idea of quality time was eating dinner, maybe watching TV or working on a puzzle. His idea of quality time had been to exercise and take a brisk walk through the neighborhood. He'd shown up again the next evening, fully suited in workout gear, with the same intentions. Shirley preferred romantic strolls instead of training sessions.

"You weren't kidding when you said Regina was going all out for Christmas." He'd taken the cue and changed the subject.

Shirley zipped up her jacket. Only about an hour of sunlight remained, but the streetlights would light their path on the way back. An hour easily passed when they were engulfed in conversation. At the beginning of their relationship, most of their talk centered around work, careers, and things happening at church. Now their conversations were more intimate and meaningful. Garrison spoke more about the future. *Their* future.

Garrison tossed a fallen tree limb from the sidewalk and into some nearby brush. "Did your family have any holiday traditions?" he asked.

"Definitely," Shirley said. Her heart warmed at the thought. "On Christmas Eve, Mama would give us our new Christmas pajamas, and we'd run to change into them and then come back to drink hot cocoa. When we finished, we were allowed to open one gift. I always chose the present that looked like a book because I didn't want to open any of the big surprises." Shirley slipped her hand into his tight, firm grip. "What about you?"

"Mama and I definitely made it a point to keep the traditions going that Pop started. Even though it took a while. Pop liked doing a seafood boil on Christmas instead of the traditional dinner."

Christmas had become a painful time of year for Garrison and his mother following the devastating loss of his father. His sudden death from a brain aneurysm when Garrison was only eleven years old stole his joy for years. He'd been bitter with God until he met a high school classmate who had also experienced the same trauma.

He helped to restore Garrison's faith in God, and he slowly but surely began to enjoy the holidays again.

Shirley felt the slight tug on her hand before Garrison said, "Let's cross the street here."

"I'm getting pretty chilly. We can go back home."

"Trust me. Let's go this way. I think someone's following us. But don't turn around," he said calmly.

Chapter Four

SHIRLEY GRIPPED GARRISON'S HAND TIGHTER. "Why would someone do that?"

"I'm not sure. But I'd rather be safe than sorry. Just because it's Christmas doesn't mean the questionable folks have taken a break. In fact, robberies go up around this time of year."

Shirley certainly wasn't carrying a purse or anything else of value on her, for that matter. She was sure Garrison had his wallet as always, but hopefully his size would be a deterrent for anyone who might have ill intentions.

"They've been driving very slowly behind us. At first I thought they were lost and looking for an address, but I'm not sure that's the case. Suspicious behavior, that's all."

"I'm nervous," Shirley admitted. Just two months ago someone had attempted to mug her while at the hospital. When it was all said and done, she was left with a slight concussion, but the culprit didn't steal anything, and the whole thing had been a diversion.

"I know what you're thinking about," Garrison said, intercepting her thoughts. "But I'm here with you."

Shirley walked in silent prayer. It was the only thing that worked to calm her enough to keep her from running away, even with Garrison by her side. It was dark now, and Shirley jumped at every shadow and rustle in the bushes even though she knew they were just critters burrowing away for the night.

"I've got you," Garrison said. "We'll stop when we get up here." They neared an intersection with a bright streetlight at the corner. "It'll subtly let them know that we're aware of their presence." He pulled his cell phone from his back pocket. "And I have a police buddy I can try to get on the phone as a precaution."

Shirley casually glanced down the street. She was too far away to tell if the car was black or a midnight blue, and she could barely see it once it turned off its lights completely. Shirley gasped as the car gunned its engine, then did a screeching U-turn in the middle of the street before speeding away. Her legs felt weak, and she fell against Garrison's chest.

"We're good," he said. "They were probably some teenagers playing around. Even if not, they knew enough not to try me. Let's go home."

Shirley's and Garrison's strides were longer and quicker than they'd been when they first left for their evening walk. When they arrived back at the house, Mama welcomed them at the door.

"What took you two so long? The temperatures have dropped quite a bit."

Garrison eyed Shirley, and she knew he wouldn't tell the complete story to her mother. He didn't want to worry her.

"We took the long way home," he said. "But here we are, safe and sound."

"Can I serve you a bowl of turkey chili?" Mama offered. "Shirley put it in the slow cooker before she left this morning, and I'm telling you it's delicious."

"Not for tonight. But I'll take a bowl to have tomorrow for lunch. I have meetings on top of meetings, and I probably won't get the chance to get away."

Mama tsked. "A big man like you needs a full stomach. I'll be right back."

"We'll keep this incident in our back pocket and only pull it out if we need to," Garrison said. "Are you going to be all right?"

"I'm fine," Shirley said. "I'm just glad you were with me."

"By your side. That's where I always want to be," Garrison said.

Shirley wanted the same thing. They'd been honest with each other before about their desire to be married. They were both in their forties. That left little room for fuzzy expectations. Even so, she was old-fashioned in that she wanted Garrison to take the lead most of the time in their relationship's progression. When she'd been the one to push for marriage in her previous relationships, they'd gone in the opposite direction.

In God's timing, Shirley thought.

"All packed up and ready for tomorrow," Mama said, returning with a container in a securely tied plastic bag.

"Thank you, Regina," Garrison said. "And I know how you feel about your containers. I'll be sure to get it back to you."

They shared a laugh. Mama never let a pot, baking dish, or container leave her house without a name label. And as promised, he returned it clean and timely—bright and early Saturday, the morning of the 5K Hot Cocoa Run. Mama, however, hadn't stirred from her sleep when Garrison arrived at six thirty to pick Shirley up. They had to be at the registration table in forty-five minutes in preparation for the eight o'clock start time for the race.

"Why do these races always have to start this early?" Shirley moaned. If she had her druthers, she would have slept in this morning. About this time, she would have been burrowing deeper into her soft plush mattress with the quilt nearly covering her head.

"When we finish, there will still be time for you to get home and climb back in your bed."

"Not likely. Once I'm up, out, and about, there's no turning back. I'll count it as a sacrifice for the cause."

"A very lucrative cause," Garrison said, as if she needed reminding.

Shirley and Garrison were welcomed at the registration table by a woman who introduced herself as Barbara. Shirley could tell by her recognizable voice that it was the same woman she had spoken to on the phone.

"Thank you both for being here on time. As you can suspect, we'll have eyes along the route to make sure that you fully complete the race without any help."

"Help?" Shirley looked up at Garrison.

Barbara shrugged. "Oh, I don't know. In case you wanted to catch a ride or something to help you to the finish line. Which I wouldn't imagine that you'd do," she rushed to say. "It's my job to make sure we protect the integrity of our part of this adventure."

"Understandable," Shirley said. "And you're right. I'd never dream of cheating. It may be fun and games, but it's still a serious matter." She attached the race bib they were given to the front of her thermal zip up. "It's official. This is my first race ever."

"Oh, come on now. What about your elementary school field days? Those were the highlight of the entire year," Garrison said.

"That depends on who you ask. You're talking to the girl who was always picked last in PE but always picked first for group science projects."

"Then it's a good thing you don't have to actually win this race," Garrison said. He planted a quick kiss on the top of Shirley's head, then tugged the knit beanie she wore down over her ears. Garrison put his hands on her shoulder and spun her around one hundred and eighty degrees. "And these ladies will be cheering us along the way."

Shirley imagined that her face probably looked as bright as the lighted star on top of her mother's Christmas tree. Joy, Anne, and Evelyn were bunched together. They were bundled up against the cold morning temperatures, but had T-shirts pulled over their outerwear that read, GO SHIRLEY, in red block letters.

"We're all in this together, at least in spirit," Joy said.

"You know we wouldn't have missed this for the world," Evelyn said.

A man wearing neon green running shoes jumped up on a nearby stage and started making announcements through a megaphone. He led the runners through a ten-minute warm-up and stretch session, then directed the runners to the starting line. Ten minutes later the walkers were directed to follow suit.

"I guess that's our cue," Shirley said to Garrison.

"See you at the finish line." Anne smiled, waving like she was sending a kindergartener off for their first day of school.

The walk wasn't as strenuous as Shirley thought it would be. At the halfway point, she stopped at one of the water stations for a brief drink, then pushed forward, keeping pace with Garrison's long and quick stride. She had to take two steps for each one of his.

"Am I going too fast?" Garrison asked, checking his heart rate on his watch.

"It's a good pace," Shirley said, trying not to huff and puff.

"Mr. Christmas would be proud of me," Garrison said. "I mentioned to him that I needed to exercise more. This is probably his way of making sure I get started."

Shirley knew how much Garrison cherished his visits with Mr. Christmas. It had become one of the highlights of both men's week. Garrison trusted not only the business acumen of Mr. Christmas, but also his spiritual wisdom. Garrison had purchased a men's devotional that they often read together, at least when they weren't playing checkers.

Garrison and Mr. Christmas were wrapped deeply in their checkers game. They hadn't heard Shirley enter. Garrison leaned forward with his elbows propped on his knees, like he was either contemplating his next move or figuring out how to prevent Mr. Christmas from ransacking his side of the board.

A man coming to the end of his life. A man in the prime of his life. A man frail with his posture bowed by age. A man with an aptitude as strong as his broad shoulders.

Shirley slid her cell phone from her waist pouch and snapped a picture, capturing the moment in time forever.

"What do you think?" Garrison asked him, using his pointer finger to slide a red checker forward.

"I think your life will never be the same."

Shirley coughed, and the men's heads turned in unison.

"I promise I wasn't trying to spy on you," she said, letting the door close behind her. "I didn't want to disturb you. The two of you look like you're in an intense game."

"About as intense as checkers can be," Garrison said. "I'm no match for him in chess. I learned that really quickly."

Mr. Christmas jumped one of Garrison's checkers. "My body may be failing me, but my mind is as sharp as a tack. Bless the good Lord for that."

Shirley's father, Charles, used to love checkers. He kept a card table and two chairs in his barbershop, and someone was always sitting there, especially on busy Saturday mornings.

"I think it's the crossword puzzles," Garrison said. "I read a study a long time ago that claimed they were linked to a sharper brain later in life."

"I'm living proof," Mr. Christmas said, tapping his temple. "A little challenge is good for the brain."

"We're almost there, sweetheart," Garrison said.

He'd slowed his pace, but Shirley knew it wasn't because he was tired. She was having trouble keeping up.

All I have to do is finish, Shirley told herself.

Motivational signs were posted along the route that said things like, "Jingle All the Way to the Finish Line," and "Dashing Through the Snow, Let's Go!" An oversized sign once they were at the two-and-a-half-mile mark said, "Light Up! You're Almost There!"

As they approached the finish line, volunteers stood on either side enthusiastically shaking red and green pom-poms, or popping cardboard cylinders that produced large, bursting puffs of fake snow. Anne, Joy, and Evelyn stood out from the crowd. They'd draped red tinsel garland around their necks and were wearing reindeer ears.

Exhilaration and pride swelled up in Shirley as she stepped over the finish line. She did it. She actually did it.

"Not too bad," Garrison said, swiping through his fitness tracker app.

"We'll do better next time."

Garrison raised his eyebrows. "Next time?"

"Sure. Why not? Maybe this should be our annual tradition."

"It most certainly should," Barbara said, interrupting their private moment. But Shirley knew her words weren't lost. Garrison caught them. She could tell by the look in his eyes.

Barbara looped orange and brown lanyards over Shirley's and Garrison's necks, then she handed them each a T-shirt, a bag of post-race snacks, and a coupon for a specialty cocoa at Two Buddies Coffee Shop.

Shirley lifted the heavy metal, which was shaped like a mug of hot chocolate, and kissed it. The metal, however, wasn't the greatest reward.

"As promised, here's what you were really waiting for." Barbara handed them a gold envelope identical to the one that had held the first clue, but this time there was also a matching gold box.

Shirley opened the box gingerly even though she wanted to rip it open like an impatient child opening her first Christmas gift. Tucked inside on a bed of velvet fabric was a cocoa mug ornament.

Shirley lifted it out, but it slipped from her cold fingers and fell to the ground, which drew a collective gasp from everyone circled around.

The ornament bounced and came to a rolling stop.

"Thank goodness it's shatterproof," Shirley said.

Garrison picked it up. "Let's pack this away safely until it makes it to the Mercy tree, where it belongs."

Shirley walked to a clearing and they all waited for the wandering runners to disperse. "And now for the next clue," she announced as she slid her finger under the envelope tab. Shirley cleared her throat. "'On the porch or by a tree, it's the perfect place for Santa's knee. Lifting voices, bright and merry. All for the man whose nose is like a cherry.'"

Shirley, Garrison, Anne, Joy, and Evelyn were silent as if they needed a moment to reflect.

"I would say the man with the cherry nose is Santa," Joy said, "but that's not necessarily true, especially through Mr. Christmas's eyes. Look around. There are a lot of red noses out here right now."

Joy was right. The chill had brightened the noses of many men.

"I say we start with jolly old St. Nick anyway," Shirley said with a shrug.

Evelyn reread the note. "I saw at least three Santas on the way home yesterday." She chuckled.

"Then we'll talk to every Santa we see."

"But what does it mean when it says it's the perfect place for Santa's knee?" Evelyn asked.

Garrison was quiet. If he had thoughts, Shirley knew he wouldn't share them. He wouldn't let a single word jeopardize their donation. He'd done his part this morning already.

"We can meet on Monday morning. Same place and same time as always," Shirley said.

"I'll have the coffee ready," Joy said.

By Monday morning, Shirley could have used two cups of coffee. Her mother had moved her decorating projects from inside to the yard outside. After Sunday's worship service, they'd left church and headed straight for the nearest hardware store to purchase the light-up reindeer that Mama had spotted in a sales flyer, outdoor twinkling lights for the bushes, and extra extension cords. Next, they shopped for decorative throw pillows for the front porch. Shirley couldn't blame her achy back or shoulders on the 5K when she was sure it was from the outside duties that she and Garrison performed while her mother directed them from behind the closed screen door.

Shirley wrapped her hand around the warm mug. She closed her eyes and breathed in the strong aroma of dark coffee beans with a splash of peppermint mocha creamer. "Mmmm. I hope this tastes as good as it smells. It smells like Christmas."

Joy joined Shirley at the table. "And I bet it will taste better with these gingerbread cookies your mom sent me. Please give her my thanks and hug her as tight as you can squeeze her."

"The more treats she gives away the better," Shirley said. "That means fewer for me to eat. I've found myself nibbling on way too many."

Evelyn and Anne arrived together, chattering away.

"Joy, it looks like we missed the memo," Shirley said when she noticed that both of her friends were dressed in festive attire.

"I had to put on something to cure the Monday morning blues," Evelyn said. "I wanted nothing more than to sleep all day." She was dressed in a green cardigan with a snowflake brooch on her shoulder that matched her earrings.

Anne wore a knitted sweater with a Christmas tree embroidered across the front and dangly ornament earrings. She reminded Shirley of a kindergarten teacher.

"And I wanted to bring some cheer to the guest services desk today," Anne said. "It's stressful to have a loved one in the hospital any time, but I can imagine that at the holidays it comes with its own kind of worries."

Anne set her purse and a women's study Bible on the table before pouring a cup of coffee. "I did something yesterday that I haven't done in all my years," she said, sitting down slowly to keep her coffee from tipping over the brim.

"What's that?" Shirley asked.

"I interrogated three Santas."

Anne told them about her Sunday afternoon. She'd approached one Santa who'd been a visitor after their children's church service and had handed out candy canes with scriptures attached. Another she'd seen ringing a bell and accepting donations in front of the grocery store. Then she'd waited in a line full of children to talk to the Santa Claus at the shopping center.

"He was like the rest of them. He had no idea what I was talking about."

"Did he at least ask you what you wanted for Christmas?" Evelyn asked.

"Of course he did. And when I told him I wanted twenty-five million dollars for Mercy Hospital, he told me I'd be better off talking to the Big Man Upstairs." Anne laughed.

"He's right about that," Shirley said. "I've been praying every day that I can solve the clues in time." She pulled the clue from her bag and placed it on the table so everyone could read it again. They stared in silent contemplation.

"At least Anne gave us a head start," Joy said. "She talked to three out of probably twenty Santas in this vicinity alone. I'm sure there are hundreds around the entire city of Charleston."

Evelyn tapped her finger on her chin. "I can personally think of three right now. The Christmas tree farm, the farmer's market, the women and children's shelter," Evelyn rattled off. "But the real question is, where are the Santas that Shirley would know about? Surely Mr. Christmas wouldn't send us on a wild goose chase looking for a random Kris Kringle."

Evelyn was right. Shirley had to admit that knowing where to find a Santa didn't often cross her mind. Her niece and nephew were beyond the age when they believed, and she didn't have daily interaction with other children. She hadn't even worked in the pediatric department for over a month. That was the place where all the Christmas magic happened.

"We should check the community calendar in the *Charleston Buzz*," Anne suggested. "If there are Santa visits around town, they're bound to be listed there. You can look and see if any of the locations would be someplace related to Mr. Christmas or where he knew you wouldn't miss it."

"Good idea," Shirley said. "I'll grab one from our break room and report back later."

"Speaking of reporting," Anne said. "Aurora is going to want an update of our finalized participation list for the Christmas tree festival."

Evelyn was the most organized of the bunch and could recall their progress quickly.

"As of last Friday, all thirty-five participants have confirmed. The tree farm dropped off the extra ten trees yesterday. Everything is in place for decorating. Once we meet with them, we should be good to go."

"Things weren't as complicated as I thought they would be," Shirley said. "The organizations that are decorating the trees are doing most of the work. Our biggest job is to make sure the logistics are in order."

"Thanks to Evelyn, that's flowed easily also," Anne said.

"Every person plays her part," Evelyn said with a smile. Her countenance dropped. "My only issue has been with a lady named Lyla Poppy. She's slightly disgruntled because her application wasn't chosen. I tried to explain to her that it was a random lottery process, but she wasn't satisfied with the answer."

Shirley remembered that name from the woman at the shop where she'd bought her mother's chenille throw. "We'll never be able to please everyone, that's for sure. You can't let it ruffle your feathers."

"Knowing Aurora, I'd say this may be the first, but it won't be the last," Joy said. "There will be other opportunities."

The ladies bid their goodbyes then hurried away to their respective jobs and departments. They'd already planned to meet again at three o'clock, the end of Shirley's shift. The official Mercy tree lighting was scheduled for that afternoon. Hospital employees and staff, even patients and their families, had been invited to place an ornament on the tree. Shirley would place the first ornament from Mr. Christmas at that time, then find the Santa that would lead to the next clue.

Chapter Five

"IT'S BEGINNING TO LOOK A *lot like Christmas, everywhere you go...*"

Shirley snapped her fingers to one of her favorite tunes. It always put her in the mood to do Christmasy things like drink eggnog, go shopping, and wrap gifts with oversized bows and curly ribbons.

"I didn't expect this many people to come down," Shirley said, gently shouldering her way through the crowd. "Folks are usually running to their cars to get home."

"I guess people are really in the Christmas spirit these days," Anne said. "I, for one, am happy to see it. It puts everyone in a much better mood, and they're a lot more pleasant when they come to guest services, that's for sure." She raised her arm and waved over Joy and Evelyn. Shirley and Anne had worked their way to the front, and a prime spot for all the action.

Shirley, honestly, also wanted to have a great view of Garrison. She loved seeing him in his role as administrator. She clutched the gift box that still had the ornament on its bed of velvety fabric.

Garrison approached the microphone stand set up near the massive live Fraser fir tree. The needles were a deep, rich green, and the scent wafted through the main lobby area as clearly as the voices of the chorale that had started singing another one of Shirley's favorites, "Let It Snow."

"I can't remember the last time I experienced a real snowfall," Joy said. "I mean the kind that comes around and sticks for a while." Following her husband's death, Joy had moved from the Lone Star State of Texas and planted her life in the Palmetto State. For the most part she'd been able to spend Christmas days wearing just a light jacket.

"I can deal with the snow," Shirley said. "It's the sleet and ice that I don't like. It's dangerous. But wouldn't it be beautiful if we had a white Christmas in Charleston?"

"Now that would be a Christmas miracle," Evelyn said.

Garrison waited patiently as the Mercy carolers performed. Shirley would have liked to join the choir this year, but she'd opted out even though they'd asked her to fill the last position. Buddy Jacobs, however, volunteered for the spot. Buddy who couldn't sing. Buddy who could barely carry a tune in a bucket. Shirley had heard his rendition of "Silent Night." It was painful, but she couldn't knock him for doing what he loved to do. Buddy's singing was music to his own ears.

Garrison began when the Mercy chorale finished the last verse. He welcomed everyone to the official lighting of Mercy Hospital's community Christmas tree. His remarks were short, sweet, and to the point, which meant one thing. He still had a full day of responsibilities, meetings, and conference calls.

At his direction, Mercy employees who had brought ornaments marched around the tree and hung them on the branches. Shirley fell in line and added the ornament from the 5K run to the tree.

"Thank you all for coming," he said in closing. "We know that some are returning home to their families and others are coming to do what we do best, and that is provide quality care to our patients. But before you leave, we have a special guest."

Garrison cupped one hand around his ear and leaned forward in dramatic fashion. The sound of jingle bells grew increasingly louder as the crowd parted to the bellow of "Ho! Ho! Ho!"

Shirley watched the expression of a young girl whose eyes bulged in surprise. Even though she'd covered her mouth in shock, Shirley could still hear her squeal of delight.

"It's Santa. It's really Santa," she said, hopping on her tiptoes.

Santa held his belly. It actually jiggled when laughed. It was as real as his snow-white beard.

"What happened to Earl?" Shirley asked. The head of Mercy's custodial staff had the same thick white hair and beard and always dressed the part as Mercy's Santa.

"I heard he had a family emergency over the weekend," Anne said. "He's supposed to be back by the end of the week. He sent a guy over to take his place. I think his name is Art."

Art passed out candy canes as he made his way to the front of the Christmas tree. They'd brought in a wooden rocking chair and a fake brick fireplace in the time that Shirley had turned her back. As a final touch, someone rolled in two stacks of fake presents and placed one on each side.

"Mommy, can I go tell Santa what I want for Christmas?" The little girl didn't wait for her mother's response but ran off— ponytails bouncing—to the front of the line. She was stopped by a red velvet rope and one of Santa's helpers.

"This is him," Shirley insisted. "What better place to have a Santa that I'd definitely find than right here at Mercy?"

She'd waved a copy of the *Charleston Buzz* in front of her friends. "None of the Santas in the paper were in places that I'd normally visit. I got so frustrated with trying to figure it out that I eventually resorted to what I always do anyway and read the local restaurant health inspection reports."

"Then we'll stand right here and wait our turn." Joy looped her arm through Shirley's, and they scooted into the line but continuously gave up their spot whenever an eager child joined. Shirley peered to the front.

"I love that rocking chair he's sitting in," Joy said. "We used to have a similar pair on the back porch where Wilson and I would sit and watch the sunset." Joy's eyes always twinkled when she mentioned her late husband.

Shirley grabbed Joy's arm. "Where did you say your rocking chairs were?

"On the back porch. Wilson faced them to the west, and we'd watch the sunset almost every day."

"More of the clue lines up." Shirley riffled through her bag. She pulled out the gold envelope containing the second clue. "'On the porch or by a tree, it's the perfect place for Santa's knee.' This is the Santa we need. I'm sure of it." She was more eager to get to the front than ever.

This time it was Evelyn who peered at the clue from Shirley's side. "'Lifting voices bright and merry.'"

As if on cue, the chorale struck up a joyful rendition of "Rockin' Around the Christmas Tree."

"Could this play out any more perfectly?" Shirley asked, swaying to the music. It didn't even matter that Buddy's off-tune singing drowned out the voices of everyone else. He was happy. She was happy. They were all happy. The ladies could hardly contain their chatter as they inched closer to the front of the line.

"Well, lookie here," Santa said, rocking back in his chair with glee. "Santa's here for children of all ages. Even the ones who are young at heart."

"Watch it, Santa," Evelyn said, wagging a finger at him. "We know where you live."

Santa tapped the side of his nose, and if Shirley hadn't known any better, she would have expected him to disappear and leave behind a snowfall of glittery dust.

"Is there something special that you ladies want for Christmas?"

"As a matter of fact, there is," Shirley said. "We were hoping you would have something that looks like this. Courtesy of Mr. Benjamin Christmas." Shirley pulled out the gold envelope.

Santa tapped the side of his nose again and wiggled it slightly. One of his helpers was by his side with a red gift bag in hand. He took the bag, waved his hand over it as if performing a magic trick, then handed it to Shirley.

Shirley immediately snatched out the mounds of green tissue paper that stuck out the top of the bag. They scattered around her feet as she reached in and pulled out a gift box and a gold envelope.

"Thank you, Santa," Shirley exclaimed. She handed the bag to Joy then opened the gift box carefully. She didn't want to risk dropping an ornament again, especially if they weren't all shatterproof. It was a wooden rocking chair with the name *Benjamin Christmas* engraved on the headrest.

"It's a nice one," Joy said. "I'd like to have one for my tree. Maybe two. One with Wilson's name and one with mine."

"That's a sweet idea," Shirley said.

Santa stood and tightened the gold buckle on his belt. Then he pulled the drawstring on his red sack and threw it over his shoulder. "I think my job here is done for the day," he said. "And remember, ladies, I know if you've been bad or good, so be good for goodness' sake."

And with that, he was gone.

Garrison walked up wearing a Santa hat. "One of the kids gave it to me. I couldn't resist."

"Then you should probably be the one to place our second ornament from Mr. Christmas on the tree, seeing that you're Santa and whatnot."

"My pleasure," Garrison said. "You're doing all the work. This is the easy part."

He placed the rocking chair near an assortment of knitted onesies and pacifier ornaments brought over by the Birthing Center.

"Hold it right there." A photographer from the media and communications department aimed his camera toward them. "Squeeze in tighter," he directed before taking a number of rapid shots. "Got it. Thanks."

"Our two ornaments from Mr. Christmas are going to need some company soon," Garrison said after the photographer walked away.

"We're working on it," Shirley said. She waved the gold envelope containing the third clue in the air. "What do you say, ladies? Another early-morning meeting?"

"Oh, I can hardly wait that long," Anne said. "Let's take a peek now."

"And I think that's my cue to leave," Garrison said. "You ladies have a blessed rest of your day." He took Shirley's hand and gave it a squeeze. "Call you later."

"I know I should be used to seeing the two of you together by now, but it still always gives me the warm and fuzzies," Anne gushed.

"Me too." Shirley smiled bashfully.

"And he's an answer to your mother's prayers," Joy said as they headed outside toward the Grove. Mild temperatures were forecasted for the remainder of the week, and everyone seemed to be taking advantage of the comfortable weather. Fortunately, there was an open table near the Mercy Angel statue, and they gathered there. Shirley pulled the clue from the gold envelope and smoothed it on the table.

"'We don't bend or break, we stand the test of time. Through high winds and battles fought, a shield of every kind.'"

"Palmetto trees," they said in unison.

"If we thought there would be a lot of Santas in Charleston, the number of palmetto trees is no comparison. They're everywhere," Anne said.

Shirley bit her lip. "We have to think like Mr. Christmas."

"I'm not sure how Mr. Christmas would think," Joy said, "but the Waterfront Park is the first thing that comes to my mind. The walkways are lined with palmetto trees."

"True," Evelyn added. "And Mr. Christmas would choose a particular tree for a particular reason. Maybe even the pineapple fountain. It's a popular Charleston site, and it's topped with a palmetto tree."

"I want to find out but not tonight," Shirley admitted. "I think a break would do us some good. This one came to us easily, but it may not be the same for the rest of them."

"That's a good idea," Anne said.

"If I go home and spend time with Mama tonight, then I can shop tomorrow, right after we go on an excursion to the Waterfront Park," Shirley said. "If anyone wants to tag along, I'd love the company. I'm still shopping for Garrison. His gift has to be special."

Shirley had been having a tough time finding a gift for him. Another necktie wouldn't do. His closet was full of them, in almost every print and shade of blue imaginable. She'd considered hiring a chef to give him a week's worth of prepped meals for when his hectic schedule didn't allow for lunch away from his desk. She'd thought it would be more heartfelt if she did that herself, but even that didn't fit the bill in her mind. She didn't know what the perfect gift was, but she would know it when she saw it.

"You sound about as bad as me," Anne said. "You would think because Ralph is such a simple man that he'd be easy to buy for, but I go through this every year. He doesn't like a lot of fanfare or fuss. Whenever I ask him what he wants for Christmas, he always tells me he doesn't need anything and I should bless someone else."

"That's not a surprise at all," Shirley said. She'd been fond of Ralph since the first day she'd met him. As their Mercy Hospital chaplain, he was esteemed throughout the entire hospital and by many people around Charleston.

"I'll come along with you," Anne said. "Between the two of us, maybe we can figure something out."

"I'll always remind you what my daddy used to say," Shirley laughed. "Two heads are better than one. Even if one is a cabbage."

"We've been putting our heads together since you got home, and we still didn't come up with anything," Mama complained. "You've shot down every suggestion I offered, and now I have a headache."

Shirley and her mother had tried to agree on a gift for Garrison over a dinner of pot roast, roasted baby carrots, and asparagus. She stood and cleared their plates from the kitchen table, then she squirted dish detergent into the sink and let the water run until it was scalding hot.

"You didn't get the headache from me, Mama. It's from all the sweets you've been eating lately. Every time I come home, you and Dot have baked up something new."

"We might be going overboard, but we don't keep nearly as much as we give away. Today we took chocolate chip cookies and peppermint bark to the senior citizens center. Tomorrow we're giving sweet potato pies to our neighbors. We should have them all baked and boxed up by tomorrow evening."

"I'll take these out for special delivery tomorrow," Shirley said. She patted the top of a stack of four boxes, sealed and tied with a green and red bow with curlicue ends. They were labeled for Anne, Evelyn, Joy, and Garrison.

"You're starting to spoil my friends."

"They deserve it," Mama said. She placed a kettle of water on the stove to prep for her evening cup of green tea. "It's my way to thank them for assisting with this mad dash around Charleston."

"They'll certainly appreciate it," Shirley said.

"Tea?" her mother offered as the kettle began to whistle.

"No, thank you. I'm going to unwind with a bath, have a delicious piece of your sweet potato pie, then read this novel I meant to start a couple of weeks ago. I received a notice from the library that it's time to renew it, and I haven't cracked it open once." She flipped through the pages, and a pamphlet from the Charleston Library Society floated out. She stuffed it back between two random pages.

"Before you do that, can you look at the wreath on the door? It's not lighting up the way it should. If one of the light bulbs is blown, it knocked out the entire thing."

"I'll take a look at it," Shirley said. She stepped out onto the porch, illuminated by the single porch light. It wasn't a faulty bulb at all. Shirley spotted the extension cord that was slightly dislodged from the outlet. She squatted down and pushed it in securely, and the wreath twinkled.

"Easy enough." Shirley reached for the porch rail to steady herself. "These knees aren't made for this anymore."

A car engine revved from the street. She hadn't noticed the vehicle before, idling with no lights. But it had announced itself, purposing to be seen *and* heard.

Shirley forgot about her aching knees and slipped quickly into the house. She peeked out the blinds. Their street was always quiet. A neighborhood of older families who for the most part didn't have children living at home but relished in visits from their grandchildren. Maybe that's who it was. Hadn't Garrison said it was probably a group of teenage pranksters?

Shirley squinted. The nearby streetlamp didn't provide enough light for her to clearly see the car under the shadowed canopy of tree leaves.

The engine revved again, and then the car edged away from the curb. Slowly. Deliberately. It gunned down the street. Shirley felt bolted in place, like her feet were weighed down in concrete. She couldn't leave the window.

"What in the world are you doing? Who's out there?" Mama startled her.

"I was looking at a car across the street," Shirley explained. "I didn't recognize who it was, but they're gone now. Nothing to worry about." She told herself the same thing.

"People always entertain more company this time of year," Mama said. "During the day, I notice quite a few unfamiliar cars. I watch them from the window too. Most of them are deliveries and such."

Shirley turned the lock and dead bolt on the front door, then peeked out the side of the curtain once more before retiring to the back. *Get ahold of yourself, Shirley,* she told herself. *You're probably making something out of nothing.*

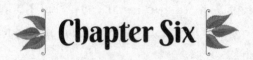

Chapter Six

"I'm telling you, Shirley, your mom is an angel. She knew exactly what I would need today," Evelyn said. She'd found a butter knife in the hodgepodge of utensils Joy kept in a drawer in the back room and cut herself a slice of pie, enough to enjoy with her cup of coffee. "Is it horrible that I'm having dessert before dinner?"

"Not at all. The horrible thing is that you didn't offer any to us," Anne joked.

"That's because you each have your own pie. There's a lot of things I'll share, but Regina's sweet potato pie isn't one of them," Evelyn said, closing the white cardboard box and retying the ribbon on top.

"Ladies, ladies," Shirley urged them. "Time is wasting."

They'd gathered once more to reread the clue and make sure the game plan was still the same. Shirley had been thinking about the clue all day. Palmetto trees seemed like the most logical answer, and they had to start somewhere.

Anne pulled on a fleece jacket bearing the Mercy Hospital insignia over her heart. "I'm saying a prayer as we speak. Hopefully the Lord will help guide us to the right palmetto tree."

Joy returned from the front register, where she'd been helping a patron find a balloon and cookie bouquet for a new mother who'd been doubly blessed with newborn twins. She put the oversized gift on a rolling cart to deliver it to the maternity ward.

"Duty calls," she said to her friends. "But I hope you find everything you're looking for. The ornament, next clue, *and* a gift for your beaus."

"Are you sure you don't want us to wait for you?" Shirley asked.

"You ladies go ahead. Sabrina is bringing Mallory and Eloise over to make slime. Slime! Of all the things we could make, they want to make slime." Joy cherished the time she spent with her granddaughters and typically acquiesced to all their requests. Shirley had joined them on occasion and gotten a kick out of making friendship bracelets, braiding colored thread into their hair, and playing with kinetic sand.

"I'm with the girls," Shirley said. "Memory boxes, homemade cards, and popsicle stick ornaments are boring. Slime is fun. The slimier the better. And glitter. If you really want to impress them, make sure you have glitter." She had taken care of enough pediatric patients to know what brought joy to their faces.

Shirley took the short walk with Anne to her reserved parking space in one of the closest lots to the hospital. To make their afternoon outing easier, they'd carpooled to work.

"I'd bet finding the next clue is going to be easier than finding gifts for Garrison and Ralph," Shirley said.

"I agree with you, Shirl. Let's go get this clue and then focus on the true scavenger hunt."

Shirley zipped her jacket to shield the cool breeze blowing off the water. The ever-present saltwater mist hung in the air, and after a few minutes she could feel her hair start to frizz at the temples.

The Waterfront Park was a picturesque postcard of perfection, especially during Christmas. White lights encircled the trunks of the palmetto trees lining the main walking path that ran along the harbor and the off-the-water walking paths.

"I bet it's gorgeous at night," Shirley said.

"Yes, it is," Anne said. "Ralph and I took a stroll the other evening. We've always loved looking at Christmas lights. When I was growing up, my daddy used to drive us through the ritzy neighborhoods to see the lights and decorations. It's one of my fondest Christmas memories."

"That's one of the best memories of a lot of people I've talked to recently. I guess we don't enjoy doing the same things we used to once we're grown up. I remember when one of the highlights of my evening was catching fireflies in a mason jar."

As they strolled, Shirley kept her eyes on the base of the palmetto trees. She didn't know if there would be a box tucked under a tree or near the brush. Her mind flipped through the numerous personal stories and conversations she'd shared with Mr. Christmas, but she didn't recall anything related to palmetto trees. He'd been able to enjoy the landscape of the beach from his room, where he could see boats dotting the water, surfers catching waves, and seagulls gliding through the sky. He spoke often of wanting to feel the warm sand in his toes.

"You know, Shirley," Mr. Christmas said.

Shirley had to stop pushing his wheelchair and listen closely to hear his weak voice. It was almost as frail as his body, which seemed to have withered over the last two weeks like an unwatered flower.

"I've always prayed that God would allow me to keep three things," he said, pausing to cough. "My health, my eyesight, and my mind. I guess two out of three ain't bad."

He looked up at Shirley. His smile reached his eyes, which, though punctuated by deep bags, were a piercing bright blue.

"You're right. Two out of three ain't bad. I guess I should start praying for the same three things," Shirley said, slowing so he could look at the leaves that had changed colors on the trees. In their time together, she'd learned what he enjoyed and what he'd come to appreciate. Nature was one of those things.

"I need someone to take me to the beach," Mr. Christmas said unexpectedly. "Do you think that's possible?"

"I can check into it," Shirley said.

"Good." His eyes grew brighter. "The feeling of warm sand between my toes is something I want to lock in my mind."

Mercy Hospital was a stone's throw away from the Charleston Harbor. Mr. Christmas's financial status afforded him the best care and attention. Shirley didn't doubt that someone would make that happen. Rarely was a request denied if it was in his health team's power to do it. It wasn't until recently that he'd requested to be moved to the private room. For his long-term care, he'd initially wanted to stay on the normal floors, stating that there was no use spending money on luxury when he was too ill to enjoy it. His son, Nicholas, had eventually convinced him that he'd worked and served others to the point that the least he could do was enjoy his money, even in what they all knew were his last days.

Shirley's clinical rotation didn't include working as a nurse on the floor with the private suites, but she'd developed a mutual affection *for him and enjoyed the time they spent together. After ninety-three years of life, his cup of wisdom overflowed. She'd even walked in several times on him and Garrison sharing private conversation and prayer.*

He believed he was born to spread the love of Christ and Christmas cheer, and Shirley absolutely had to make sure one of his last wishes was fulfilled this year.

Anne and Shirley walked for about twenty minutes with no luck. Shirley made eye contact and spoke to every passerby, in case they were one of Mr. Christmas's helper elves. Most returned a jolly "Happy holidays" or "Merry Christmas" and went on their way. Only one frazzled gentleman stopped. Holding an empty leash, he asked if they knew the whereabouts of his runaway puppy.

"I feel sorry for him," Shirley said once he'd hurried away. "I hope he finds his dog."

"It's a horrible feeling. Remember when Eloise and Mallory's puppy, Mopsy, ran away? We all looked around for him for an hour only to find out he'd run across the street and went through the neighbor's doggy door when they weren't at home. They found him curled up on a dog bed in the laundry room."

Shirley shook her head. Those were the kind of disasters she was afraid of. Since summer her mother had been mentioning that she wanted a dog to keep her company. Shirley knew her mother could benefit from the companionship and unconditional love, but on the other hand Shirley knew that pets were a lot of work. However, with every word, her mother chipped away at her resolve.

"Mama wants a dog. She's ready for it, but I'm not sure if I am."

"You should give some serious thought to it. I don't think it's a decision you'll regret." Anne slowed their walk as they approached the third path. "How many trees have we looked at so far?"

"It seems like hundreds," Shirley said. Her feet were screaming for an Epsom salt soak. "Let's circle around to the fountain. I nearly forgot about the palmetto tree on top of that statue."

"I did too," Anne exclaimed. "We probably should've started there."

"At least something good came out of it," Shirley said. She tapped her fitness watch and opened the app that recorded her steps. "I exceeded my daily goal."

As they rounded the path, Shirley noticed a young lady dressed head to toe in a green one-piece outfit. Shirley assumed she was about college aged. The middle of her shirt was decorated with an oversized red sequined ornament that sparkled from the reflective lights of the streetlamps above her. The soles of her shoes flashed whenever her feet stomped the ground.

"It looks like our clue awaits us," Anne said.

"That's definitely our girl," Shirley said, excitedly. She was even more sure when the girl tapped across the screen of her phone and a Christmas carol filled the air. Other people stopped to watch her sidewalk show. "'It's beginning to look a lot like Christmas, everywhere you go…'"

Shirley looped her arm through Anne's, and they swayed through the rest of the song. It was a good feeling to know she was on her way to the third clue that quickly.

Shirley and Anne applauded louder than the other onlookers once the show came to an end. "That was amazing," Shirley said. "I'm Shirley. Shirley Bashore," she emphasized. "And this is my friend, Anne."

"Nice to meet you," the girl said, playfully giving a bow. She stooped and riffled through a duffel bag that had been tossed in the nearby grass.

Shirley had expected her to pull out the gold gift box and envelope, but instead it was a red blinking ball on a piece of elastic string. She snapped it on her nose, finishing the look with a pair of reindeer antlers.

"My goodness," Anne said. "It's an entire production. Mr. Christmas outdid himself with this clue."

"Or maybe not," Shirley said. She took a step closer to the young lady. "Would you happen to have anything to give to us?"

"Oh sure!" Her eyes lit up. "Let me get that for you right away." She dug in her duffel bag once again and produced a black permanent marker and a receipt. She scribbled an illegible word on it and punctuated it with a smiley face. She repeated her actions on another scrap of paper and handed one to each of the ladies. "There you go."

Shirley furrowed her brows, sure that the look on her face matched the expression on Anne's.

"What's this?" Shirley asked.

"My autograph," she said, sliding on a pair of mittens that looked like reindeer hooves. "I thought that's what you wanted."

Shirley eyed Anne incredulously.

"Charlie in Charleston," the girl said, as if her name alone would clear up Shirley's confusion.

"We're sorry," Anne said. "I don't think we're as hip as we should be."

Shirley chuckled. "We're definitely not *hip* if we're using words like *hip*."

"Not to be rude," the girl said, "but could you kindly step to the side? I need to finish my Christmas video challenges. I'm posting them to social media. You should look me up. I'm almost up to half a million followers."

"Then we'll hold on to these autographs for good measure," Shirley said. "And are you sure you don't have anything in that duffel bag of yours for us? A gold envelope and a gold box?"

"Nothing like that at all," she said, taking a few steps back. "In fact, this is starting to feel a tad bit creepy."

"Oh no. Please. We're leaving now," Anne said. She grabbed Shirley's hand, and they moved as fast as they could in the direction of the famous pineapple fountain. "The last thing I want is for us to go viral," Shirley said when she caught her breath.

"Can you imagine? Ralph and Garrison would be horrified."

"And my mother would never let me live it down," Shirley said. Though dusk had begun to settle, people still roamed the area or sat on park benches.

When they reached the pineapple fountain, they walked its perimeter. Twice, to be on the safe side. A third time to ensure that if one of the park visitors needed to see them, they'd be easy to spot.

"I think we struck out," Shirley admitted. "We'll have to put our thinking caps on."

"What do we do now?" Anne asked.

"Well, if you're still up for some shopping, we can head over to the shops near Waterfront Park or the Harbor. We'll have plenty of time to find the next clue. There are eight left and twelve days to find them. We have plenty of time."

Shirley enjoyed spending a few hours with Anne, and they browsed the unique and handmade gifts that many of the hometown and boutique shops had to offer. She added to Dot's eclectic earring collection, purchased a cordless coffee mug warmer for her nursing supervisor, and a Baby's First Christmas ornament for a nursing colleague who'd recently returned from maternity leave. She even found several trinkets for herself but nothing that tugged at her heart for Garrison.

"Do you think he'll like it?"

Anne handed over her gift for Ralph to be wrapped. It was a handmade solid oak watch box with a brass plate that she would have his name engraved on. Inside she'd tucked a note that read, *"Our love will forever stand the test of time."*

"I don't think he'll like it at all," Shirley said then paused for effect. "I think he'll *love* it."

Bells tinkled on the door to the shop, announcing the arrival of more patrons. Their local public broadcast stations and the city's politicians had been encouraging the citizens of Charleston to buy locally for Christmas, and it seemed like their public relations push was working.

"Yoo-hoo, yoo-hoo!"

Shirley would know that voice anywhere. She didn't recall ever seeing Aurora in jeans, and she looked years younger with a long cardigan sweater that danced down at her calves and her hair pulled up in a high ponytail.

"I was walking by and couldn't let you two get away," Aurora said to Shirley and Anne.

Truth be told, Shirley didn't want to talk about the Christmas tree festival or anything related to Mercy Hospital at the moment. She truly only wanted to enjoy her time with her friend and continue looking for a gift for Garrison before her mother started hounding her about what time she'd arrive home for the evening.

"Hi, Aurora," Anne said. "Are you out shopping as well?"

"A little bit here and there." She covered her mouth as if she was telling a secret. "I saw something at the shop a few doors down the other day that I wanted to get for myself."

"There's nothing wrong with that," Shirley said. "I'm guilty too."

"But I don't want to bore you talking about my Christmas purchases. I wanted to make sure you knew that we've decided to add two things to the Mercy Christmas tree festival. A holiday market leading up to the culmination of a hot chocolate toast on Christmas Eve."

Shirley bit her tongue. She, Anne, Evelyn, and Joy comprised the entire committee, and she knew for sure they'd never discussed additional events. Obviously the *we* Aurora spoke of didn't include them.

"Would you mind if we held off on the details until tomorrow?" Shirley asked.

Aurora looked taken aback, but she didn't push the issue. "Sure. I guess that was kind of rude of me to interrupt your time together with talk of business. Tomorrow it is," she said. She tapped her watch. "I suppose I should be headed out anyway if I don't want to be late."

"You look nice. Where are you going?"

"To the Fort Moultrie Visitors Center. They're having a dessert reception and showing of *A Christmas Carol* in the theatre where they usually show their documentary films. I never get tired of visiting there during the year. It's rich with history."

Shirley had learned very quickly upon coming to Mercy that Aurora was a history buff.

"Sometimes we forget about our own city's history," Anne said.

"That's true," Shirley agreed. "I don't think I've been to the forts since the field trips in elementary school."

"You should visit again soon, especially since both Fort Sumter and Fort Moultrie have been designated as national historic parks," Aurora said. "I learn something new every visit. I mean, I just learned that palmetto tree logs were used to build the actual forts and defend our harbors."

"Wait a minute. Say that one more time."

"The original forts were built from palmetto tree logs because they could absorb the shock of the cannonballs."

"Are you thinking what I'm thinking, Shirl?"

"Most definitely," Shirley said. "Is this event open to the public, Aurora?"

Aurora dug in her purse and produced a brochure, then handed it to Shirley. "Of course it is. As a matter of fact, they're showing a different Christmas classic every day this week. Here's a list if you're interested."

"I'm definitely interested. In fact, I'm so interested that I'm going tonight."

"I'd love to have the company," Aurora exclaimed.

"We'll meet you there," Anne said, rushing toward the door.

Shirley started out behind her, then turned back to Aurora. "You don't realize what you did, but you'll find out soon enough."

Shirley and Anne reread the clue before heading into the Fort Moultrie Visitors Center. *We don't bend or break, we stand the test of time. Through high winds and battles fought, a shield of every kind.*

A modest crowd had gathered inside. They mingled quietly and enjoyed the display of colorful petit fours and other sweets set out on a table. Soft instrumental music played in the background. They were a reserved crowd, Shirley noted. They looked studious, the kind that would bury themselves in classic novels and reference books for entertainment.

Shirley observed the people in the room, looking for the person in charge.

"Over there, Shirley," Anne whispered. "He's the only person I see wearing a badge." Her eyes were set on a tall, lanky man wearing a deep green sports jacket and pair of khakis. He had a handkerchief tucked in the front pocket but no tie.

"We should probably stay and watch the movie first. I don't think it would show good manners to eat and run, so to speak." Shirley bit the edge of her lip.

"You're probably right," Anne agreed.

The microphone rumbled with static when the man Anne had spotted stepped up to it. He tapped it with his finger first then cleared his throat.

"If everyone can find a seat in the theater, we're ready to start our showing of *A Christmas Carol*. If you're a Scrooge and would like to leave early after eating our treats, please hurry and make your way to the exit now so we can begin without disruption."

"Well, we definitely can't leave now," Shirley whispered to Anne.

They followed the flow of the crowd into the theater and grabbed the two end seats on the back row. Aurora shuffled past them and plopped down beside Anne.

"You never told me why you wanted to come tonight of all days," Aurora whispered. She was holding a brownie in her hand and picked two walnuts off the top. Her mouth dropped open. "I bet this has to do with the Mr. Christmas's wild adventure, doesn't it?" She placed her hand over her heart. "I cracked one of your clues, didn't I?"

"Possibly," Shirley said. She ignored the irritated glare of the woman sitting directly in front of her who turned around to stare them down. "You may have led us to our next ornament and clue, but we can't be sure yet. We'll have to wait until the movie ends."

Aurora pointed at the man who'd made the announcement. Shirley had been right. He was the man in charge, and his name was Walter.

"This is exciting," Aurora said.

Shirley wasn't sure if she was talking about the clue or the movie. She zipped her finger across her lips and turned her eyes to the screen as the overhead lights dimmed. Shirley felt antsy, but she had no choice but to settle in to watch the past, present, and future of Mr. Ebenezer Scrooge. She was tired. So very tired.

Shirley felt a slight nudge on her arm. She sat up straight. She hadn't meant to doze off in the middle of the movie.

"Shirley, it's time to go," Anne whispered as the lights rose in the small auditorium.

"What happened? Why are they stopping the movie?"

"Because the movie is over."

"Oh my goodness," Shirley said. "This is embarrassing."

"At least you weren't snoring," Anne said. "I didn't have the heart to wake you. You've been on your feet all day. Trust me, no one noticed. Not even Aurora."

"It's a good thing we snagged these seats on the back row," Shirley said. She waited for everyone from the other rows to file out before bringing up the rear.

"Please grab one of the desserts on your way out. Most of our treats tonight were made by Poppy's Sweet Shoppe. You can pick up one of her business cards on the way out."

"Lyla is a busy woman," Shirley said when she recognized the name. "She is definitely doing what she can to market her new business."

"Maybe this opportunity was enough to keep her off our backs," Anne said.

Walter offered them a brochure and firm handshake as they passed him. "It's always nice to see new faces," he said. "I hope you come visit us again, and I hope you enjoyed the show."

"It's one of my favorites," Shirley said. It was true, despite her nodding off for the majority of the movie. "And I'll definitely come back again."

Walter squinted his eyes. "You look familiar, but I can't place your face."

"I'm Shirley Bashore." Shirley never thought she'd be the kind to throw her own name around, but the circumstances called for it. "Maybe you've seen me at Mercy Hospital. I'm a nurse there."

Walter shook his head. "Fortunately, that's one place I haven't been to in a long time. No offense."

"None taken." Shirley laughed. "No need to be a frequent visitor or patient to a hospital if you don't have to. Count it a blessing."

"Maybe you have a common face or look like someone I know," Walter said.

"Did you attend the party at the Christmas mansion a couple of weeks ago?"

"I wasn't fortunate enough to go this year, but I have in the past. Can you believe Mr. Christmas would volunteer here every now and then? Of course it was years ago when we were both much younger and had hair." He chuckled. "A man of his stature could've just written a check, but he gave of his money and of his time."

"I'm not surprised, knowing what I know about him," Shirley said.

"I was sad to hear about his passing," Walter said.

"He did leave a little of himself behind," Anne said, steering the conversation in the direction that Shirley needed her to. "I'm sure you've heard about the challenge he issued."

"I can't say that I have." He scratched his temple and held his hand out directing them toward the door. Shirley took it as their cue that he was ready to go home, wanted them to leave, or both. "I'll be looking for you two again," he said, then walked away.

A janitor pushed a dust mop along the floor from one end to the other. He moved quickly, like his wife had a hot dinner plate awaiting his arrival. Shirley jumped out of his path since he rushed toward her like he'd run over her instead of going around her.

"I'm sorry to bother you," Shirley said. She couldn't leave yet.

"Uh huh," he said, without looking up at her.

Walter fiddled in his pocket for the key to unlock a drawer at the front desk then dropped his name badge inside. He used the same key to open a narrow closet near the desk. He hung his sports jacket on the single clothes hanger inside. As he knelt and changed out of his loafers, Shirley spotted it. The gold box with the matching envelope.

"Excuse me," Shirley said, pointing at the closet. "I think that belongs to me."

Walter followed the direction of her finger. "That?"

"Yes," Shirley said, "the box and the envelope. Who do they belong to?"

"I'm not sure." His long arms reached the top shelf with ease.

"It's for me," Shirley blurted out. "I'm nearly certain of it."

"Why would it be?" Walter asked. "You said yourself that you hadn't been here since elementary school." Walter drew the items into his chest, shielding them from Shirley and Anne. "What do you mean it's for you?"

Shirley took a deep breath and outlined the challenge Mr. Christmas had given her with Anne chiming in agreement.

"I promise you every word I said is true. Is there anyone you can call about it? There has to be someone else who put it there."

"Excuse me for a moment," Walter said. He picked up the phone receiver on the desk, punched the numbers furiously, then turned his back. He still seemed wary, but hopefully he was calling someone to corroborate their story.

"There were some items in the front closet that need to be identified. Do you know anything about them?" Walter looked over his shoulder with a suspicious eye. "Yes, that's correct. They're both gold."

His shoulders relaxed, and Shirley and Anne smiled at each other.

"Okay, I see," Walter said into the phone. He turned slightly toward them. "Let me double-check." He turned fully to Shirley and Anne. "I need to see your license, please."

Shirley reached into her purse and produced both her license and hospital ID badge. "Like I said before, I'm Shirley Bashore, and this is my friend Anne Mabry. We're both employees at Mercy Hospital, and Mr. Christmas issued a challenge that I have to complete in order for Mercy to receive the donation he left behind in his will." She spoke loudly, hoping whoever was on the other end would hear.

"Show him the other clue envelope," Anne urged.

Shirley pulled out the envelope containing the other clue, nearly ripping the edge in the process.

Walter eyed the two envelopes.

"I've got it from here," Walter said to the person on the other end of the phone. He hung the phone on the base with force, making Shirley jump.

"Sorry, I never knew about this. My coworker tucked it in that closet over a month ago and forgot all about it until yesterday. You know what they say. Out of sight, out of mind. I haven't noticed it all this time. You have quite an eye on you."

"I'm a nurse. I've been trained to pay attention and spot things others miss," Shirley said, gladly accepting the envelope.

Walter shoved his hands in his pocket. "You should probably know, my colleague said that someone tried to claim these items yesterday. That's why I asked to see your ID."

"My goodness. Who would want to do that?" Anne asked.

"Evidently someone who doesn't want Mercy to get that money," Walter said. "I'd be careful if I were you. The world isn't how it used to be."

Shirley and Anne scurried to the car as fast as they could. Shirley wondered if they were being watched. Had the person who tried to claim the clue been there tonight? Was it possible that it was whoever was in that dark car she'd seen following her and Garrison, then again in front of her house?

"I'm kind of creeped out," Shirley admitted. "I feel like someone is lurking out there."

Anne started the car and threw it in reverse. "We're not going to stick around to find out."

They didn't open the gift box until they were parked safely in front of Shirley's house. Anne clicked on the dome light in the car so they could see the ornament clearly. It was a palmetto tree and crescent moon encased in a clear shatterproof ornament.

"How nice," Anne said. "It looks like our state flag. This is my favorite."

"I should let Aurora put it on the tree tomorrow," Shirley said. "She's the reason we found it. If not for her, we may have been searching around every palmetto tree in Charleston."

"That's an excellent idea," Anne said. "Now to the next clue."

Shirley ripped open the envelope tab with less care than she'd done the others. She pulled out the slip of paper and read it aloud. "'We don't mind digging deep with our fingers and hands. Playing here is better than castles in the sand. If you have a lot to give or perhaps nothing at all, a humble gift to our Savior is never small.'"

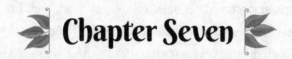

Chapter Seven

SHIRLEY DIDN'T KNOW HOW MANY more pictures Aurora expected her to take. She'd excitedly accepted the offer to hang the palmetto ornament on the Mercy Christmas tree, but somehow it had become an entire production.

"Shirley, could you change it to a black-and-white filter before you take the next shot?" Aurora asked. Her hair had been twisted into a messy bun when she'd first arrived, but since coming down from her office to the lobby, she'd let her tendrils fall down in loose waves. Somehow Shirley had turned from a nurse into a photographer.

"That's beyond my scope of knowledge. You can edit it later though."

This photo shoot was eating into Shirley's lunchtime with Garrison.

"I think I've taken the perfect shot," Shirley said, handing Aurora her phone. "Here you go."

"Glad to be of help last night," Aurora called out behind her. "Even if it was unintentional."

Garrison was waiting for Shirley in his office with two Greek salads full of vegetables with olive oil on the side like she'd requested.

"You didn't have to wait for me," she said, sliding into the high-back chair across from him. She waited for him to gather a set of papers and toss the stack in the inbox at the corner of his desk. She'd never seen him make it to the bottom of the inbox before.

Garrison stretched his hands above his head, then intertwined his fingers and rested them behind his neck. "I need to take a lap or two through the halls of Mercy. I've been sitting in this chair all day. My joints feel—and probably sound—like the tin man."

Shirley covered his desk with napkins then flipped open the plastic tops to their trays.

"One day you're trying to fatten me up with sweet potato pies, and the next day you're feeding me rabbit food," Garrison said.

"It's good for you. I need to keep you around as long as possible."

"Is that so?" Garrison said.

He gave her *that* look. The one that made her blush like a teenager who'd gained the attention of her crush.

"It's not that easy to eat healthy around here at Christmastime," he said. "You can't imagine how many sweets are delivered to this floor on a regular basis. I keep the fruit baskets and cheese and crackers, but I send the rest of it to the break rooms throughout the hospital."

"No wonder I run into temptation no matter where I am," Shirley said.

"Mm-hmm." Garrison swiped a napkin across his mouth. "This rabbit food isn't too bad."

A light tap on the door interrupted their conversation. Julie, Garrison's administrative assistant, peeped in. Not counting Shirley's closest friends at work, Julie was the first to notice the growing relationship between her and Garrison. Julie would sometimes catch them in whispered conversations in the hallway, or share the awkward elevator ride up from the main lobby when they tried to hide the fact that they were more than colleagues. Now it was common knowledge. Old news. They were no longer the talk around the water fountain. At least their relationship wasn't. But lately Shirley couldn't walk the corridors without someone making a comment.

"We're depending on you, Shirley."

"How are things going?"

"If you need any help, let me know. How's the old guy gonna know anyway?"

"Garrison is really going to love you if you pull this off."

Julie placed four bottled waters on a side table that already had a tray stacked with individual packs of trail mix, peanuts, and shortbread cookies.

"I'll be out of your way in a few seconds, Mr. Baker. I wanted to drop these things in here before your meeting with the Christmas family. I need to run to a doctor's appointment, and then I'll be right back."

"Thank you," Garrison said. "It slipped my mind already." He wiggled his mouse, and the screen of his computer monitor came alive. It opened to his calendar, busy and color-coded. "I want you to take your time with your appointment and be sure to grab something to eat for yourself, but do you think you'll be back before the board meeting at three?"

"Most definitely, barring any unforeseen circumstances. And I already have lunch. I picked up something when I ran out to get your salads. I'll see you guys later," Julie said.

Shirley waited until Julie eased the door closed before she questioned Garrison. "You're meeting with the Christmas family? You never mentioned that."

"It was a last-minute thing. They called today to see if they could get on my schedule. I really don't have the time, but I feel obligated."

"Why are they coming? Have I done something wrong?" Shirley had been careful to make sure she stayed within the stipulations.

"No, no. From what I know, you're fine. They said they're interested in seeing a list of proposed capital improvements and programs where we plan to allocate the funds if we receive the donation."

"If?" Shirley raised her eyebrows. Where was Garrison's confidence in her?

"When," Garrison corrected himself. "*When* we receive the donation."

"I thought what Mercy did with the money was left to the discretion of the administrators and the board since there were no specifications to how the money was to be allocated."

"You're right," Garrison said, slowly and quietly, the way he did when he didn't want to stoke her fire. "We don't have to get anything approved by the Christmas family, but I agreed to the meeting as a courtesy. I don't think there will be any harm in it."

Shirley swallowed her irritation. He was right.

Another soft tap interrupted their conversation.

"Come in, Julie," Garrison said. He took a bite of his salad.

The door opened slowly, but Shirley didn't realize they had unexpected company until Garrison stood. He flipped his necktie from over his shoulder where he'd tucked it while he ate, then tightened the knot.

"I apologize," the man said. He was dressed in black from head to toe, making his carrot-colored hair seem more prominent. "I didn't see anyone sitting out front, so I found my own way." He gestured to the placard outside the door bearing Garrison's name. "Easy to find."

He entered the room with no regard for Shirley's presence or the obvious fact that they'd been enjoying lunch.

"I'm Tatum Everett III. I'm here to represent the Christmas family. My father, Tatum Everett Jr., is the estate-planning attorney for the Christmas family."

Shirley easily saw the resemblance. They shared the same deep-set eyes and high-tufted hair along their receding hairlines.

"I didn't realize they'd be sending a representative," Garrison said.

"My fiancée, Madeline Christmas, stepped out to take a phone call."

Shirley shot Garrison a glance as she gathered their half-eaten salads and crumpled napkins.

"I apologize," Tatum said, as if he'd just noticed Shirley. "I always arrive at least thirty minutes early for my appointments. My father always taught me that to be early is to be on time, to be on time is to be late, and to be late is to be forgotten. And I never want to be forgotten."

"Your father made sure that wouldn't be possible," Shirley said, extending her hand. "Shirley Bashore."

"Ahh, Shirley. I didn't recognize you."

"Glitz and glam on a nurse is a far cry from these scrubs and clogs," Shirley said. "I don't remember meeting you the other night."

"I arrived later than I intended. A dinner meeting with a client held me over, and I missed the big announcement. Now I get to meet the woman who stole my would-have-been great-grandfather-in-law's heart. He put an awful lot of trust in you. You should be honored."

"I am," said Shirley. "Honored now but slightly horrified at first."

Tatum rocked back on his heels. "Tell me—how is this whole little challenge thing going?" He circled his hand in the air as he said the words, as if he didn't take it seriously.

Little challenge thing?

"It's coming along. My friends and I have solved three clues."

"Only three?"

Was that a smirk? "Three is better than none," Shirley said with a laugh she couldn't even convince herself was sincere.

The youngest Tatum adjusted his turtleneck. "It's a slow-moving process, I see. Time waits for no one."

Shirley didn't need to be reminded. "I have faith that everything will turn out the way it's supposed to," she said to Tatum.

"Good luck to you then," he said. "You're definitely going to need it."

His words pricked at her. It was like he didn't want them to succeed. Either that or he thrived on his pessimistic personality.

What Shirley didn't mention was that she was already a step ahead with the next clue, or at least half a step. Fingers crossed. Joy had a hunch she wanted to follow, and it hit her as soon as they'd read the clue earlier that morning.

"I'll leave you two to handle business. Tatum, nice seeing you today, and I'm sure you'll be there when the check is presented to Mercy Hospital from the Christmas family."

"You can only wish," Tatum mumbled.

She left Garrison's door ajar. A woman whom she'd seen at the party but hadn't officially met was having a hushed phone conversation in the corner. She looked up as Shirley approached and offered a pleasant smile. Her bright ice-blue eyes—the color of her great-grandfather's—twinkled in the same way.

Shirley hadn't meant to eavesdrop on the conversation, but she picked up bits of the conversation as she walked past.

"I'm not sure why he's doing this. I really don't need the money. I'm beginning to think Papa Ben was right about him."

All the Christmas grandchildren clan called him Papa Ben. Shirley slowed her steps and hoped the elevator was as slow as it always was.

"Look, I have to go. But I'll call you later."

Shirley slipped into the elevator after the doors slid open. At first impression, Madeline didn't seem to be the kind of woman who would keep company with a rude man like the one Tatum Everett III had shown himself to be.

Shirley didn't have time to tell anyone about her run-in with Tatum until the friends met later that evening.

"He really rubbed me the wrong way," Shirley said.

"Don't let it get the best of you, Shirley," Evelyn said. "We're making more strides than he knows because we're about to get another clue tonight."

"I've really been wondering if Madeline was talking about Tatum. Do you think he's trying to get his hands on the Mercy donation?"

"How can he?" Joy asked. "Besides, she wasn't necessarily talking about her fiancé. They're a wealthy family and surely have money staked in countless places. She could've been commenting on a business partner or venture."

"I guess you're right," Shirley said, though she wasn't entirely convinced.

They quieted their voices as they entered the Charleston County Public Library, following Joy's hunch. The librarian at the front greeted them with a nod, then turned back to a stack of books she'd been scanning. It was quieter than usual in the main area, even for a library. Almost eerily so. Shirley didn't know if college students still studied in the local libraries, or high schoolers for that matter. Her niece and nephew didn't even carry textbooks in their backpacks anymore. Everything was electronic, even their report cards and transcripts.

Joy pushed open the door to one of the meeting rooms down the hallway, and they walked into a flurry of activity. Six tables were lined in two rows, spaced wide enough that people could easily walk between them. All the chairs had been pushed against the wall, leaving room for the busy attendees to work while standing.

As a woman who loved flowers, dirt, and all things green, Joy's face was lit with enthusiasm. "I know we're here to seek out a clue, but I've been looking forward to putting these wreaths and garlands together. Every now and then I'm bitten by the creative bug."

They wrote their names on a sign-in sheet and went to the last empty table as directed by the woman overseeing the activities. Tonight's activity was to make wreaths and garlands that would be used to decorate area nursing homes and senior living facilities. They could choose from evergreen wreaths, Magnolia wreaths, a holiday evergreen cross, or a garland.

"Instructions and printed examples are located on each table," she said. "Or feel free to use your creativity."

"I'll tie the bows," Shirley said, rolling out a spool of red and gold satin ribbon. "All those years of tying big fancy bows on Cynthia's and my Easter dresses will finally pay off."

"I can handle that too," Anne said.

Shirley scanned the room looking for Claudia Guest, Joy's neighbor and the founder and president of the Petals and Plants Garden Club. Joy was sure that the fourth clue had something to do with gardening. Shirley had read until she had it memorized: *We don't mind digging deep with our fingers and hands. Playing here is better than castles in the sand. If you have a lot to give or perhaps nothing at all, a humble gift to our Savior is never small.*

"Playing in the dirt is just as satisfying as playing in the sand," Joy had told her. "It's the second part of the clue that's got me stumped. We'll find out soon enough if Claudia has our next clue in hand."

And the sooner the better, Shirley thought. Claudia had never looked like a play-in-the-dirt kind of woman. Joy confirmed her predictions when she said that the Petals and Plants Garden Club actually did more talking and researching about plants than they did actually growing and propagating seeds. Over ten years ago when Claudia lost her bid to become president of the more prominent Garden Club of Charleston, she started the pet project so she could have something—and maybe more importantly, some people—to be in charge of.

Per usual, Claudia was poised as a picture of perfection. Or as Mama used to say, "Dressed to the nines." Everyone else was dressed in casual comfort, but Claudia wore a silky pewter-colored blouse, red slacks, and low red heels. Her chin-length bob was tucked behind her ears, showing off a pair of flashy teardrop earrings. Tonight, she was being the face of the organization and definitely not the hands.

"There's Claudia," Shirley said to Joy.

Joy was spreading garland down the length of the table and had gathered a collection of pine cones and red berries. "Hmm?" she said, lost in her own thoughts. She turned a sprig of berries back and forth as if trying to find the perfect position.

"Claudia," Shirley said again.

Joy finally looked up. "Don't you worry. She's making her rounds."

Joy was right. While Shirley and Anne tied ribbons, Joy worked on securing pine cones and berries to a garland, and Evelyn secured ornaments to a wire they planned to weave through a wreath, Claudia floated her way to the table.

"I couldn't be more thrilled to see a group of Mercy ladies," she said, clasping her hands under her chin. "You've done so much for me lately, I'll have to figure out a way to return the favors."

"Return the favors?" Anne asked. "What do you mean by that?"

"Well, obviously for coming tonight," Claudia said. "But especially for making sure Petals and Plants was included on the list to showcase Mercy's Christmas tree festival. I tell you, what we have planned will absolutely knock your pantyhose off. I know those are coveted spots. I personally know someone who is mad as a wet hen about it."

"We had so many people interested that we had to choose the participants randomly," Evelyn explained. "I guess you can say it was the luck of the draw and you were one of the ones that got the long end of the stick."

Claudia sang her words. "If you say so." She turned to Joy and gave her a wink. "Your secret is safe with me."

Joy looked at Shirley and shrugged. Nothing they said would change Claudia's mind. It wasn't worth trying to convince her otherwise.

"And look at you, Shirley. I thought you'd be running around town finding clues for the great Christmas challenge. What brings you here tonight?" She stopped and cupped her hand over her mouth. "Oh my goodness. Do we have one of the clues?"

Chapter Eight

Shirley deflated. If Claudia wasn't aware of the coveted gold envelope and box, then the answer to the clue wasn't what Joy thought. Shirley could see that the disappointment on her friends' faces matched what she felt.

Joy put down the pine cone she'd been holding. "Would you happen to be pulling our leg, Claudia?"

"Let me tell you, twenty-five million dollars is nothing to play about. If there was anything I could do to make sure Mercy receives a substantial donation, I'd do it without a second thought. I wish I knew something, but unfortunately I don't have a clue. Literally."

Claudia looked over their heads and waved her hand in the air like a pageant queen riding in a homecoming parade. "Looks like I have a visitor from the Garden Club of Charleston. I better hurry along to see to what I owe the pleasure of this visit. I've been making quite a name for myself in the gardening community. They're probably here for advice," she said, whisking away with short, quick steps.

"I'm sorry, ladies. I was so sure," Joy said.

"We still need to decipher the last part of the clue. Maybe that will help," Evelyn said. "Tell us one more time, Shirley."

Shirley perfected a knot on a white bow with red polka dots as she repeated, "'If you have a lot to give or perhaps nothing at all, a humble gift to our Savior is never small.'"

"What could we ever give to a Savior who was born just so he could give His very life for us?" Anne asked.

The ladies turned when they heard the tinkling of a bell. As the room quieted, they spotted Claudia up front. She waited until all activity stopped and it was quiet enough to hear a pin drop.

"Ladies." She turned to acknowledge the only male in the room. "And gentleman. We've been asked to help the Garden Club of Charleston with distribution of their poinsettias this year. They've doubled the amount they usually receive and would like to brighten the day of the elderly in the community. They received a list of addresses for seniors who regularly visit the senior citizen center. We have the names up front in case anyone is willing to deliver the poinsettias to those in your own neighborhoods."

Shirley decided to check the list on the way out. Her mother's name was probably there since she was a frequent visitor to the senior citizens center.

"If you'd allow me a moment, I'd like to read this card from the president of the Garden Club. 'Thank you to the members of Petals and Plants Garden Club for your selflessness. My mother, God rest her soul, always loved poinsettias. She gave them to her friends and family members every year, and always placed potted poinsettias around the altar at church over the holidays. During this Christmas season, I encourage you to read the story of the poinsettia. It will be a blessing.'"

"The only thing I want to read is the next clue," Shirley whispered. "We've got to think smarter. Even though Tatum was rude, he was right. We don't have much time. We're going to have to step it up."

"We're right here with you," Evelyn said. "Mercy is going to get our donation if we have to search every nook and cobblestone cranny in Charleston."

"Tomorrow we'll be refreshed and ready," Shirley said, unspooling more ribbon. "But for now, let's enjoy ourselves."

The ladies put their frustrations aside and focused on creating five wreaths and three garlands that looked as professional as the decor sold in stores. Several people came by to admire their work, including Claudia, who eyed their creations with fondness.

"Impressive," she remarked. "And will you be able to take a few poinsettias for delivery as well?"

"Yes," Shirley said. "I'm sure my mother and her good friend Dot are on that list. They go to the senior center every week, especially when it's Bingo Day."

"Then your mother likes prizes," Claudia concluded. "We also have a gift bag we're sending. The things inside aren't Bingo prizeworthy, but there are items I think she'll appreciate."

As Shirley predicted, there were poinsettias waiting for her mother and Dot. The garden club had also thoughtfully left behind big cardboard boxes that could be used to carry the flowers to prevent them from tipping over during transport. She agreed to deliver five poinsettias, including three others that belonged to members that attended church with her at Mother Emanuel.

"Oh, look at those," Mama exclaimed as Shirley muscled through the door, carefully moving inside with the box. "Are all of those for me?"

"One of them," Shirley said. "The others are for Dot and three ladies at the church. They're gifts from the Garden Club of Charleston and the Petals and Plants Garden Club."

"How nice." Mama eased a poinsettia from the box and studied the tips of the petals. She stuck her finger down in the soil, then rubbed a pinch between her forefinger and thumb. "This one needs water."

"I'll give all of them a little drink." She handed her mother a red gift bag. "More presents."

Mama peeked inside. "Fuzzy socks. And they're my favorite kind. They have the rubber grips on the bottom. They're good for old folks like me." Next she pulled out a pack of lemon drops. "I like to put these in my hot tea," she said and kept rummaging through the bag.

"It's a *Christmas* gift. You don't want to wait and open it on Christmas Day?"

"Not particularly," Mama said. She pulled out a card. "I'll read this and put the rest of the things back."

Shirley peered over her shoulder. "What does it say?"

"I can hardly see it without my glasses," Mama said, handing the card to Shirley.

"It's the story of the poinsettia," Shirley said. "I don't know how they expect anyone to read it without a magnifying glass."

"Oh, I can tell you about that." Mama made her way to her favorite armchair and eased down. She pointed to the couch across from her and signaled for Shirley to take a seat.

"Some people say that the leaves are shaped like the Star of Bethlehem that led the three wise men to baby Jesus. And the red leaves represent the blood that He shed for us on the Cross. It's the life of Jesus in an entire plant. But that's only part of the story. A Mexican storytelling tradition tells of a poor young girl who only had weeds to offer as a gift on the altar on Christmas Eve. Legend says when she laid the weeds at the feet of baby Jesus, they turned into bright red flowers."

"That's beautiful," Shirley said. Her mother had never shared that story with her before.

"And do you know what made her gift special? It came from a humble heart."

Shirley sat up and leaned forward. "Wait, what did you say?"

"Which part? I said a lot if you were listening." Mama stood and walked toward the box of poinsettias. "Now, can you get a cup? I want to water these little babies before they start to droop."

"One second, Mama," Shirley said. She looked around. Where had she put her phone? She patted the pockets of her scrubs. Nothing. She dumped the contents of her purse. Nothing. She went outside and checked in the small crevices between her car seats. Nothing.

She walked back through the evening in her mind. The last time she'd used her phone was for GPS to calculate the distance between her house and her church members'. She must have left it somewhere near the registration table or on one of the rolling carts they used to load the poinsettias. There was nothing she could do about it now. She would have to wait until the morning to call and see if someone turned it in to the library's lost and found.

Shirley needed to call Joy and ask her if the Garden Club of Charleston had an actual office, but without her cell phone, Shirley didn't know Joy's number. Since she'd logged it into her phone, she'd never taken the time to memorize it. Or even Anne's and Evelyn's numbers for that matter. She needed to tell them how the clue made sense.

Digging in dirt was as fun as digging in the sand, hence the garden club. Joy had been right with that piece. But the second part about having little or nothing to give but still bringing a humble gift to the Savior was a nod to the poinsettias. Where had the garden club purchased them?

"Why are you running around here like a chicken with its head cut off?" Mama asked. She'd finally gotten a cup, pulled a funnel from the kitchen junk drawer, and was done watering the poinsettias.

"I was looking for my phone. I need to call Joy, but unfortunately I don't have her number memorized."

"That's an easy fix. Look in the drawer under the telephone for a notebook with flowers on it. I keep all the phone numbers I might need in there."

"How do you always have what I need when I need it?" Shirley asked.

"Because that's what mothers do," Mama said with satisfaction.

Shirley pulled out the drawer and looked under a stack of coupons, pushed a pack of batteries back, and lifted up a handful of ballpoint pens. When she pulled the drawer out as far as it could go, she finally found the book of stamps she'd been looking for the other day, but no flowery notebook.

"Mama, it's not here. Any idea where you might've put it?"

"That's strange," Mama said, slowly shuffling into the kitchen. She stared into the drawer like doing that would make it magically appear.

Shirley shrugged. What was the point? "Don't worry about it. I'm headed to bed."

"I'll be behind you shortly. I want to stay up for the news and see what's happening with the weather."

"Still dreaming of a white Christmas?" Shirley asked, and she followed her words with a loud yawn.

"I still have eleven days to hope," Mama said, going back to the gift bag from earlier. "I need those socks now. My toes are cold."

"Daddy always complained about you putting your cold feet on him," Shirley remembered as she headed down the hallway to her room. Her memories of her parents' love were just as clear as if they'd happened the day before. Her father used to hide a pair of cozy socks in her mother's stocking every year. Shirley had forgotten about that. But whether she wore socks or not, her mother's favorite thing to do was to tuck her feet under the bend of her father's knees as they relaxed on the couch.

Before Shirley could close her bedroom door, the doorbell rang. "Who's that, Mama? Are you expecting anyone to stop by at this time of night?"

"Not at all," Mama answered.

Shirley slipped her feet back into her bedroom slippers and went out front. She peeked through the window and, seeing no one, was hesitant to open the door. What if it was the same person who had been trailing her and Garrison?

"Who is it?" Mama asked. "Maybe it's Eulene. She mentioned earlier that she was going to drop off a fruitcake."

Shirley looked in the direction of Eulene's house. Eulene had been her mother's neighbor for at least the last thirty years. Her house was completely dark, which could only mean one of two things. Either she was with her son and she hadn't returned for the evening, or she'd retired for the night.

"Eulene's house doesn't have any lights on."

"Then it's probably a delivery. You know this time of year the drivers are working overtime to make sure their deliveries are done each day."

"But I didn't order anything," Shirley said. She peered down the street. "And I'm sure you didn't either."

"But Cynthia always mails her Christmas gifts, so I'm often on the watch for them." She nudged Shirley out of the way and turned the lock on the door. "The last thing I'd want is for someone to take off with a box she's sent. She sends nice, expensive things, you know."

When Mama opened the door, there was a boxed poinsettia on the porch identical to the ones they'd received from the Garden Club of Charleston. Shirley stepped outside and frowned when she thought she smelled pipe smoke. As she lifted the box, she saw a black SUV pull slowly away from the curb, U-turn, and drive away in the opposite direction.

Shirley brought it in and set the box on the coffee table. She lifted the poinsettia out and found a gold envelope with her name on it. Mama reached in for the gold box that always accompanied the clue.

Chapter Nine

"I'm not sure why it was delivered directly to my door, but I'll take it however it comes," Shirley said on Thursday morning as she stood in front of Mercy's Christmas tree with Joy, Anne, and Evelyn. "Maybe it was supposed to make its way to my home with the other poinsettias but things somehow got mixed up."

"Then write it off as a Christmas miracle," Anne said.

"I believe Mr. Christmas put a lot more thought and effort into his last hurrah than we would have thought," Evelyn said. "Remember how his letter mentioned that he felt like he knew *us* because of *you*, Shirley? I bet he did a little research on us too. I'm sure he knew about Joy's participation in the Petals and Plants Garden Club."

"He did. I even had Joy make him a flower arrangement from her garden to brighten his room. One thing about Mr. Christmas was that he always had a very astute mind, even for a man his age."

When he was well enough, Mr. Christmas enjoyed being pushed around the lobby at Mercy, admiring the commissioned artwork in the gallery, visiting the display of Mercy memorabilia that had found a permanent spot after the Memories on the Harbor exhibit, sometimes sitting silently outside in the grove by the Mercy Angel. Even though he'd been ill, Mr. Christmas was the one who made sure to encourage Shirley. She treasured the richness of their conversations, and strove to give him everything he asked for, which wasn't much. He had come to value experiences over possessions.

"Where are you taking me?" Mr. Christmas asked.

"Now, sir, you aren't going to put up a fuss, are you?"

"Not with my favorite nurse," he said. "I just didn't expect a field trip today."

"Sometimes the best trips are the unexpected ones." Shirley draped two cotton blankets on the back of the wheelchair in case he needed them, and after making sure he was comfortable, she placed an insulated lunch bag on his lap. "Hold on tight to that."

"Does anyone else know that I'm leaving? They told me this morning that I was supposed to have a scan around this time."

"But since you ate breakfast there's been a change of plans. They moved it to the morning. They need you to do a CT scan with contrast. You'll have to fast four hours for that. So sit back and enjoy the ride."

Mr. Christmas did as he was told, and soon they stopped under an open blue and white striped beach umbrella. Shirley's arms ached, and it had taken more effort than she had anticipated, but she would do it a million times over if she had to.

Mr. Christmas wanted to put his toes in the sand, and since it was within her power to help him fulfill that wish, she had committed to getting it done. She and Garrison had planned to go out to lunch today, but this was more important. Garrison had set up the umbrella for her and she'd brought along two fruit salads for her and her patient to enjoy. Garrison stood on the dock.

"Mr. Christmas, are you all right?" Shirley asked, walking around to see him.

Tears streamed down his face, and he dabbed them away with the back of his hand as Shirley bent over and pulled off his hospital-issued footies. She folded up the footrests on the wheelchair and set his feet onto the sunbaked sand. He wiggled his toes, and for the first time since they'd met, Shirley saw Mr. Christmas cry.

"Shirley, are you okay?" Evelyn asked, interrupting her walk down memory lane. "Did you hear what Joy said?"

"Uhh…no," Shirley said, adjusting the poinsettia ornament that had been with the last clue. Her mother had gotten a kick out of being the only one to share in the moment.

"Claudia texted her and said they found your phone in the ladies' room at the library. She recognized you from your screensaver. She's coming by today to decorate the Petals and Plants Christmas tree for the festival, and she's going to drop it off to me when she arrives. I'll make sure you get it first thing."

"I mostly miss my phone for two reasons," Shirley said. "I want to make sure that Mama can reach me if she needs to, but I also missed my daily good morning texts from Garrison. Sometimes it's a simple 'thinking of you,' or even a 'God has great plans for you today.'"

"Your entire demeanor lights up whenever he's around," Evelyn said. "And to think, you almost let one of the good ones get away."

After a failed work relationship and messy breakup in her past, Shirley had been hesitant to date anyone at her place of business. But Garrison was humbly persistent, and her heart softened to the possibility of a relationship with him.

"I told him about my theory for the next clue, and he agreed to go along with me. But with no assistance whatsoever," Shirley rushed to say. "He's along for the ride."

"You'll love it. Ralph and I went last year, and the view was breathtaking," Anne said. "I've got a thing for Christmas lights anyway, but to see the lights of all the shops, houses, and other passing boats as we floated along the harbor was picture perfect."

"I'm looking forward to it," Shirley said. "We haven't had much time together alone lately, but this is the perfect night to steal away. Mama is actually spending the night at Dot's house because they have the rehearsal for the church's Christmas play this evening."

"If I'm available, I'll be there to see her," Joy said. "Don't forget to remind me."

"Sure thing. I'll pick up some extra tickets."

"Let's see that clue again, Shirley," Anne said. "I have a few minutes before it's time for me to begin my patient deliveries. I want to get as much done as I can before the discharges begin. It's been really busy over the last few days."

Shirley reached into the pocket on her scrubs and pulled out the piece of paper with the clue on it. She read it slowly and clearly, pausing to emphasize certain words. "'It may be up for sale or merely to admire. Oftentimes the scenery changes; it's something they require.'"

"That's definitely the dinner cruise," Evelyn said, nodding. "I'm convinced of it. Earlier this year there was an article in the

Charleston Buzz about the current owners looking to sell the yacht. They were ready to retire to Florida, and the generation behind them didn't want to take over the family business."

"I remember that article," Anne said. "The city was also considering having it declared as a historic landmark so it could be a tourist attraction."

"Exactly. And the dinner cruise takes a different route each time, which means the scenery changes. It even changes as they cruise along. Makes sense to me."

"We've been wrong before." Joy bit her lip.

"But we're getting the hang of things," Shirley said. "If nothing else, at least I'll have a romantic dinner with Garrison tonight." Suddenly a light bulb turned on in Shirley's mind. "And you know what? Mr. Christmas told me that he proposed to his wife on a yacht. I remember the story because he talked about how drenched they got when it started to rain when they were on the top deck."

"No rain expected in the forecast tonight," Joy said. "Go get that clue."

Shirley and Garrison stood atop the open-air observation deck on the three-story yacht. Temperatures hovered in the low forties in the early evening, weather that normally would have kept her inside. But tonight was special in more ways than one. Shirley was glad she'd chosen the black knee-length sweater dress, fleece-lined leggings she'd been waiting to wear, and leather boots. Silver hoop earrings and a silver bangle topped off her look. She rested in the crook of

Garrison's arm and leaned back comfortably against his chest as they stared out over the calm, rippling water. Christmas lights from nearby buildings reflected across the water.

"It looks like fireflies dancing on the waves," Shirley said.

"What do you know about fireflies? We called them lightning bugs."

"I know that they stink if you put too many in a mason jar." Shirley laughed. "Cynthia and I would poke holes in the lids with my daddy's screwdrivers. We were young at that time. It probably wasn't the safest thing for two children to be doing."

"That was called living," Garrison said. "If today's parents allowed their children to do some of the things I did, they'd be called unfit."

"All of that unfit parenting and you still turned out okay," Shirley said.

"Just okay?" He chuckled. "I'll take that."

Another couple joined them on the deck, though the woman wasn't dressed nearly as warmly as she should have been. Her silk blouse blew with the breeze and she wrapped her arms around her waist. Then she hid behind her significant other to try and shield herself from the wind. He was tall and slender and no help to the cause.

Garrison pulled Shirley closer. "It's harder for me to keep my mouth shut than I thought. I'm like everyone else around. I feel like I need to help you."

"You're helping by being here." She eyed the couple beside her suspiciously. It seemed like they'd wandered closer to them. Or was it her imagination? "Like I told you before, I always feel like someone is watching me when I'm out clue hunting."

"I think I can confidently say that Mr. Christmas wouldn't have anyone track you who had the intent to do you harm. He wasn't that kind of man."

"You're right," Shirley said, turning back toward the stairs that lead to the main deck.

Garrison easily slipped his hand into hers and assisted her down the steep incline. A seated dinner would be served in fifteen minutes, and attendees were starting to find their seats among the tables. Garrison pointed at the table located closest to the heating source. Although the large dining deck was enclosed, the atrium windows still gave them a dazzling view of the harbor. She'd made the reservation in her name, so whoever held the clue would know she was on board tonight. If they'd been pulled into the adventure, they'd have to have their eye on every passenger and check the diners' list thoroughly.

Both Shirley and Garrison started their dining experience with Charleston she-crab soup and a seasonal house salad. When Shirley had called to make the reservation, the hostess had bragged about the gourmet dining experience, but even with that, the chef's talent exceeded Shirley's expectations. And to think they were considering closing the family business.

A man approached their table wearing a black suit with a sprig of holly pinned to the lapel. He conversed with the couple sharing their table, then approached Shirley and Garrison.

"Good evening, I'm Bernard, the dinner captain extraordinaire. How has your experience been tonight?"

Shirley noticed how he eyed their plates. Garrison had eaten all but a bite of his pork chop marinated in sweet tea, but she still had a sizeable portion remaining of her Low Country shrimp and grits. It was enough for her to save for her mama for the next day's lunch or enjoy tomorrow for her own dinner.

"Everything was delicious," Shirley said. "I was very impressed. I have to admit this is my first time dining on this particular boat."

"And hopefully this won't be your last."

Shirley raised her eyebrows. "No more thoughts of closing?"

"I see you also read the *Charleston Buzz*," Bernard said. "It'll be a few years before they make a final decision. The owners are still stowing away to Florida for retirement, I'm afraid, but at least their family has agreed to help keep the business afloat. Pun intended."

"What changed, if you don't mind me asking?" Garrison placed his flatware on his plate, and out of nowhere a waiter appeared to clear his setting.

"This is the part that should be in the *Charleston Buzz*," Bernard said, taking it upon himself to slide into the empty seat beside Garrison. "Have you ever heard of a local philanthropist named Mr. Benjamin Christmas?"

Garrison sat forward in his seat although he didn't respond. He knew his role. He was here to accompany Shirley, but he wouldn't jeopardize anything by uttering a single word.

"I'm familiar with him, yes," Shirley said.

"In his will, he left a substantial donation toward the business because he proposed to his wife while aboard this very ship. It wasn't a dining location at the time. Back then it was used for entertainment for the more affluent citizens of Charleston. He couldn't stand to know that the ship would be permanently docked. Of course, he's already sailed away on the great ship in the sky."

"He certainly has," Shirley said, not really knowing what to say about the awkward phrasing. "Shirley Bashore," she said, extending a hand. "And this is my Mercy Hospital colleague, Garrison Baker."

Bernard was forthright. "From the way you two were staring in each other's eyes, I would've pegged you to be more than colleagues." He elbowed Garrison like they were old friends.

Shirley smiled pleasantly, but she refused to be roped in by any conversation that didn't have to do with the initial reason for her visit. "So if you're familiar with Mr. Christmas, then you may have heard about the donation that he allocated for Mercy Hospital."

"No, I haven't. Was it in the *Charleston Buzz*?"

Shirley went on to explain the charge she'd been given. Word usually got around fast in Charleston, but she was finding that this was moving slowly.

"Now that sounds exciting. How can I help? Should I call in the crew to search for a clue on the boat?"

"Not exactly," Shirley said. "If a clue was here, someone would probably already know about it."

"And that someone would be me," Bernard said. "I'm in charge of operations on the boat. I would know, but it wouldn't hurt for me to ask around. Give me a few minutes."

Shirley tried to act nonchalant as she watched Bernard question the employees as they collected empty plates, refilled empty glasses, and served desserts. They turned to glance at her, and soon Shirley realized she'd become not only the talk of the staff but of the guests too.

Bernard returned with a sampling of desserts but nothing else. "I wish I could help you, Ms. Bashore, but no one seems to know a thing." He pushed the dessert tray in her direction. "Please accept these on the house. I hate that you didn't get what you came looking for."

"We were in good company tonight," Garrison spoke up. "That counts for something."

"You know what?" Bernard said. "I'm feeling the Christmas spirit, and I know when I see love in the air. You can't trick me with that colleague comment." He bowed at the waist. "Your entire meal is on the house. We'll credit the prepayment back to your card. A Christmas gift from us to you. Enjoy the rest of your night."

Shirley reached across the table for Garrison's hand. "The evening wasn't wasted at all. I enjoyed my time with you."

"Even though I'm a colleague."

"You know you're much more than that." Shirley spooned off the corner of a piece of cheesecake and tasted it. Soft and creamy. She was stuffed after dinner and hadn't believed she could eat another bite, but she somehow found room for something so delicious.

The remaining hour of the cruise passed quickly as Shirley and Garrison took in the beautiful sights of the Low Country. There was a specialness to seeing it at night and illuminated by thousands of lights—twinkling white in some places and colorful as rainbows in others.

As they disembarked and walked to the car, Shirley finally let reality set in. "I hope the ladies aren't disappointed in me. We don't have time to make many more mistakes."

"I've heard it said that mistakes are the portals of discovery," Garrison said. He tugged her arm, slowing her fast-paced walk down the sidewalk. "Think of the mysteries you and your friends have helped solve over the last year and a half. Not to downplay this one, but they were more difficult than this."

Garrison was right. Shirley had been swept into being an amateur sleuth almost since she'd walked through the doors of Mercy Hospital. They weren't quitters.

"Now think of Mr. Christmas," Garrison said after they'd climbed into the cab of his new F150 pickup truck. He blasted the heat and turned on the seat warmers. It was piping hot in no time. "He would want you to have fun. He loved this city and the people in it. He wants fun for you too."

Shirley peeled off her overcoat and even her boots temporarily. She loved the feeling of the heat warming her toes. "You're right. I should find the fun in it all."

She was pretty sure it would be easier said than done.

Chapter Ten

"Garrison makes a good point," Joy said. "We're going to find the fun in all of this."

Shirley sat down at the circular table in the back room of the gift shop. They'd gathered for lunch and to also join Anne for one of her favorite Christmas pastimes—writing Christmas cards. Shirley remembered when her mother used to receive so many Christmas cards that she had enough to hang them around every doorframe in the house. Slowly over the years the numbers dwindled down in those she received and gave.

"It's nice to get something in the mail other than bills, solicitations, and coupons," Anne said, dropping a handful of ballpoint pens in the middle of the table. "I call it happy mail."

"I definitely want to spread some Christmas cheer," Evelyn said, sliding into her seat with a midday cup of coffee to top off her lunch. "This is nice. Thanks for the idea, Anne. Believe it or not, these are the same ones I intended to send out last year." She tapped the unopened box of greeting cards.

Shirley opened the first box of cards she'd purchased with the manger scene against a starry night background. She jotted down a list of the people she wanted to send greetings to—her nursing friends back in Atlanta, ladies from one of the Atlanta homeless shelters she'd served at once a month, and family members. She hadn't spoken to some of her cousins since last year this time, but that didn't lessen the love between them. In the new year, she'd vow to do better.

Based on her list, Shirley knew she wouldn't be able to finish every card during lunch, but she would write some after work too. Her mother finally found her notebook of scribbled phone numbers and addresses, and she wanted to join in on the fun as well.

Although Joy's volunteer, Lacy, was out front assisting guests, Joy stuck her head out occasionally to see if she could offer help to customers. She'd been gone for a while before she reappeared at the back door with someone by her side.

"Look who I found Christmas shopping in our gift shop," Joy said, pulling the woman into the doorframe.

Abrielle Fleury, the proprietor of Belina House Gallery, managed the gallery display of paintings in the hallway leading to the emergency room. Shirley appreciated learning about the local artists of the artwork Abrielle procured.

Abrielle blew kisses at all of them from the break room door. "I don't want to interrupt you ladies. I'm peeking in to say hi." She lifted the shopping basket hooked on her wrist. "And to purchase these. I was only coming in for a pack of mints and saw these hand-woven bracelets and more of my favorite hand-poured candles. I tried to walk away, but I couldn't. I don't know any hospital gift shops with items as unique as these."

"I try my best," Joy said.

Shirley wasn't sure what the gift shop had looked like before Joy took over, but it had been transformed into a place where even the physicians and staff frequented. It was a vibrant—yet peaceful—corner of the hospital.

"I missed you last month," Joy said. "I look forward to you telling me the stories behind the artists and their work when the artwork in the gallery is changed out."

Abrielle's blond hair was slicked back into a low bun. She wore a red blouse with an oversized bow tied perfectly at the neck, fitted navy slacks and dainty gold earrings shaped like anchors. Abrielle supervised the exchange of artwork from the Belina House Gallery each month. She worked alongside her sister, Claire, at their family house near the cobblestoned Queen Street. A painting from their family collection of Dr. Arthur Fleury, one of Mercy Hospital's founders, hung in Garrison's office.

"I believe I worked myself to the point of exhaustion," Abrielle exclaimed. "I was going back and forth to Savannah to help another gallery. Claire insisted that I take a break during November, and she even took over planning our Thanksgiving dinner."

"It's nice to see you again," Shirley said. "I can't wait for the new display. You never disappoint."

Abrielle smiled. "Thank you for your kind words. I need to run along before Grey starts texting me. Sometimes I feel like I'm on an electronic leash," she said, speaking of her assistant, Grey Monte.

"Lacy will take care of your purchases. I'll have to come by and see you soon at Belina House," Joy said.

"Don't be a stranger. That goes for all of you," Abrielle insisted. She hugged Joy and air-kissed her cheeks.

"I'm adding the Fleury sisters to my list of Christmas cards. Shame on me. I'd forgotten all about them," Joy said once she was back in front of her growing stack. She stuck personalized returned labels to the left corner of each one. "God put a special prayer on my heart to include in their card."

"While you're at it, can you say a special prayer for Aurora too?" Shirley asked. "Every chance she gets, she's chasing me down about the holiday market. She cornered me in the elevator when I was taking a patient in for a CT scan and wanted to know if we'd sent in our graphic design request for the table placards and then asked if we've secured entertainment for the hot chocolate toast on Christmas Eve."

"Why can't we take the easy way out and use prerecorded music?" Evelyn asked. "My niece added a Christmas playlist to my phone, and I'm sure the audiovisual department can figure out how to transfer it from my phone."

"Because Aurora insists on live entertainment," Anne reminded her. "I thought about asking Steve, the high school band teacher, if the jazz ensemble would be available, but then I remembered the students will be out for holiday break by then."

"It's still worth a try," Shirley said. "Sometimes they can participate in activities for extra credit. I know that because one of the nurses in the heart center has a son who plays saxophone."

"Then I'll call Steve. He's a member of our church and sometimes comes to our small group." Anne had pushed her cards aside and pulled out her notebook where she kept a checklist of the event planning logistics. She scanned the list with her finger. "I've been putting off calling back Lyla Poppy. Again."

"Again is right," Shirley said. "I'll give it to her for persistence, but at this point she needs to accept that there's no space for her this time."

For the last four days they'd been hard at work planning the holiday market and unfortunately had run into the same problem. There were too many interested businesses and not enough vendor spaces. They'd also decided not to have too many businesses who sold similar items, and unfortunately for Lyla Poppy, they didn't need any more food vendors who sold baked goods and candies.

"I agree. People are going to have to be more understanding," Joy said. "If we—"

Joy was interrupted by the sudden sound of chaos coming from outside the gift shop.

Crash! Whoop! Yelp!

It was followed by a prolonged chorus of jingling bells.

"What in the world is going on out there?" Evelyn asked, leading the way out of the gift shop. Shirley was curious but cautious. Her father had always taught her that if you ever heard or witnessed disruption, to run away from it instead of toward it. But the moment she stepped out of the gift shop, Shirley nearly lost her footing as a fluffy blur barreled toward her. It ran between her legs, dragging a rope of bells behind it.

Shirley fell against the wall but thankfully didn't lose her footing. Dr. Barnhardt wasn't as lucky. The dog stopped and turned in a circle in an attempt to free itself from the tangled rope of bells. He jumped onto Dr. Barnhardt's chest, knocking a cup of coffee out of his hand. What didn't land on the floor caused a flowering stain across the front of his white physician's coat.

"Oh great," he grumbled. "Now we have loose dogs running through the hospital."

Seamus McCord, head of security, leaped over the spill and weaved through the human obstacle of guests and staff as he rushed by in pursuit of the furry blur.

"Sorry, sorry, excuse me," he yelled out as he pushed by.

"Not only loose dogs but loose security guards," Shirley said. She eyed Dr. Barnhardt apologetically. "You're a mess. But of course you already know that."

"I'll grab an extra pair of scrubs," he said, shaking his head. "You'll vouch for me while I go get cleaned up?" he asked Shirley.

"Sure thing." They had been working side by side in the emergency department all morning. Shirley hadn't had to attend to anything too critical thus far. A man came in who'd broken his ankle after missing a step on the way down from a ladder while hanging lights outside. From the time he was rolled in, he and his wife had been having whispered arguments about why she had to have Christmas lights hanging from the gutters anyway. Then there was the feverish child with a tummy ache, and an elderly woman with an unidentified itchy rash across her torso. All in a day's work.

The hospital's main lobby was getting more action than the emergency room. Too much action.

Shirley couldn't believe her eyes. An entire row of Christmas trees had fallen over. They were leaning on each other like fallen dominoes. Ornaments were scattered across the floor, and loose pine needles littered the area. Shirley was thankful they'd instructed everyone to use shatterproof ornaments, or else there would be a real mess.

"We're not going to be able to fix this without help," Shirley said.

"A lot of help," Evelyn said, shaking her head.

Calls would have to be made to people from the participating organizations to come and recreate their Christmas tree magic. Shirley counted the trees. Thirteen. Thirteen had toppled. The last tree had fallen against Claudia's from Petals and Plants Garden Club, but somehow it was still upright.

Claudia's Christmas tree featured a collection of lifelike petunias, zinnias, and a pinkish flower Shirley didn't recognize. She'd figured out a way to attach hummingbirds with a clear twine to give the appearance that the birds were hovering over the flowers. Most of the organizations wanted to stand out amid the crowd and typically avoided anything that looked traditional. It was all about being as unique and original as possible.

Shirley and Evelyn found Joy snapping pictures of the toppled trees. Anne was on the phone, her face etched with worry.

"Could you send someone up from the maintenance or custodial department to help straighten the trees?" she was saying. "And we'll also need bins to put the ornaments in until we can make contact with all the organizations. I'm sure they'll want to rehang the ornaments themselves." She paused, and relief washed her face as she listened to whoever was on the other end of the phone. "You're the best."

Anne dropped her phone into the front pocket of the smock she wore to protect her clothes. "Of all things that could've happened, who would have imagined this? I saw that same stray dog sniffing around outside this morning."

"Here's the culprit now," Shirley said.

Seamus had wrangled him up and calmed him down enough to lead him outside. He had a rope loosely looped around his neck as a makeshift leash. "There you go, boy. Let's go outside until we find somewhere for you to go."

"Poor fella," Shirley said, watching the dog's shameful eyes as he passed. It was almost like he knew he was the cause of the entire debacle. "Since the excitement is over, I better hurry back to the emergency department."

She headed past the bank of red elevators and the gift shop and down the hall, where Abrielle was using painter's tape to secure protective paper around the recently removed paintings leaned against the wall.

"Thank goodness we weren't in the middle of exchanging the paintings when the pooch ran down this way." She dropped the roll of tape in a canvas work bag.

Shirley didn't notice Abrielle's assistant, Grey, standing nearby until he spoke. "This is a nice change of scenery," he said. "If only I'd been blessed with artistic talent. But I only get to admire what others create."

His words sounded an alarm in Shirley's head. *It may be up for sale or merely to admire. Oftentimes the scenery changes; it's something they require.* She knew she should have been hurrying back to the emergency room, but she couldn't return until she asked some questions.

But once Shirley saw the latest painting being carefully hung, the questions answered themselves—a painting of a stately and ornate mansion that exuded Southern hospitality. The mansion of none other than Mr. Benjamin Christmas and his family. Had

Shirley never stepped foot inside, she would have imagined that the patriarch who lived there was stuffy, pretentious, and a bit austere. Yet Mr. Christmas had been none of those things.

"Abrielle," Shirley said, "please tell me you know something about a gold envelope and a matching box."

Chapter Eleven

CLAIRE SAT BEHIND HER DESK at the Belina House Gallery. She'd been snacking out of a small bowl of cashews when Shirley arrived to meet the sisters following the end of her shift. Abrielle had doubted that anyone at the Belina House Gallery knew anything about a clue, but one call to her sister back at their family-owned art gallery proved her wrong.

"I'm shocked. I can't believe I knew nothing about this," Abrielle said. She stood in front of her sister, an incredulous look covering her face. She'd been wearing a pair of black oversized shades to filter the bright sunlight that shone despite the cool temperatures. They now doubled as a headband to keep her wispy blond hair from her face.

"Number one, you were on a much-needed break from all things related to work and I didn't want to bother you," Claire said with a flick of her hand. "Number two, let's be honest. You would've let the cat out of the bag. I didn't want you to spill the beans."

Shirley stood between the two women, her gaze bouncing back and forth like she was watching a tennis match.

"I guess the only thing that matters is that you have what you're looking for," Abrielle said to Shirley.

"And that Mercy Hospital is one step closer to getting that money." Claire clasped her hands in excitement. "Now I can stop watching for you to come in every day. I even temporarily changed my volunteer hours at the gift shop so I wouldn't slip up and tell Joy."

"And you say *I'm* the one who would've let the cat out of the bag?" Abrielle shook an accusatory finger. She crossed her arms then turned her attention back to Shirley. "Well, can we see?"

Shirley instinctively clutched the items to her chest, but after seeing the women's disappointed faces, she tucked the envelope under her arm and maneuvered the gold box with both hands.

"I guess there's no harm in showing you the ornament. All of them will be hanging on the Mercy Christmas tree for the public to admire anyway."

Shirley opened the lid and handed it to Abrielle then slipped a single finger in the ribbon loop of the ornament. It swung on the end of her finger.

"Wow! Look at that," Claire said, leaning in for a closer look. "It's an exact replica of the painting of the Christmas family house that we hung in the gallery today."

"Even down to the ornate frame," Abrielle added.

Shirley held the ornament at arm's length. The colors were as bright and vibrant as the original.

"Mr. Christmas has truly outdone himself," Shirley said. "I wonder who he chose to create the ornaments. They're all unique."

Abrielle and Claire nodded in agreement.

"So what's next?" Abrielle asked.

"Next I hang this on the tree at Mercy and get started on the next clue. It's a race to the finish line. There are still five clues left. Five clues and nine days."

"Oh my," Claire said. "Is there anything we can do to help? We'll close the gallery and run all around the city if we have to."

"That's sweet of you, but I have all the assistance I need. Actually all of the assistance that I'm allowed to have."

Shirley explained further when she saw the puzzled looks on their faces.

"Then it seems to me you have everyone you need," Abrielle said. "You ladies are sleuths extraordinaire. I've never known a Mercy mystery that you couldn't solve, and you know we know that firsthand."

Shirley pulled out her phone as she made her way back toward the hospital. It was within walking distance, and the brisk pace helped her to sort her thoughts. She sent a group text to get everyone up-to-date.

Mission accomplished. Headed back to hospital now.

Evelyn was the first to respond. Meet you in the lobby.

The lobby was a flurry of activity, as some people had already returned to redecorate their toppled trees. With Evelyn acting as supervisor, all was neat and orderly. At her friend's request, maintenance had secured the bottom of all the trees with sandbags, and an employee from Evelyn's department was passing out a collection of tree skirts to cover the base of those who didn't have their own.

"Now if we can keep the stray animals from having a field day through here," Shirley said.

Evelyn directed a rolling cart containing a bin of wayward ornaments to the end of the row of trees. Two women waited to pick through it.

"Seamus was able to take our furry culprit to the animal shelter," Evelyn said. "Maybe someone will take him home for Christmas if he doesn't already have a family who comes to claim him."

"He's a rowdy one. He needs to be in a house full of children." Shirley laughed. She held up the gold box and shook it lightly. "You're going to love this one."

Evelyn oohed and aahed just like Shirley thought she would. She couldn't believe the intricate details down to the light sconces on the portico that seemed to emit real light.

"Thank goodness our Mercy Christmas tree wasn't damaged," Evelyn said as Shirley reached for the tip of a branch high above her head. Although she hadn't clustered all the ornaments from Mr. Christmas together, she wanted to keep them in the same section where they could be found easily when she came to admire the tree. She would have liked Garrison to join them, but as usual, Julie said he was stuck in a meeting that would undoubtedly drag on for the remainder of the day.

"And now this." Shirley pulled the clue out of the envelope. She'd been patient and hadn't opened it in front of the Fleury sisters. "'A loving, caring home is something that's not minor. Take pause and offer a life that could be finer.'"

With a quick flip of the wrist, Evelyn twisted her hair to the crown of her head and secured it with a clip shaped like a seashell. It matched the brooch pin on the lapel of her heather-gray blazer. Evelyn reread the clue in a low whisper.

"I'm free all day tomorrow, Shirley. My Saturday belongs to you. Should we meet at my house in the morning?"

"That sounds like a plan. I'll be there at nine."

"Perfect." Shirley felt her phone buzz in the pack she wore around her waist. It was a text from Garrison. ON A QUICK BREAK. IF YOU'RE STILL HERE I'LL WALK YOU TO YOUR CAR.

Shirley texted back. I'D LOVE THAT. MEET ME IN THE LOBBY. I'LL BE IN THE TREES. She thought for a moment than texted again. I'M ALWAYS AROUND WHETHER IT'S CLOUDY OR SUNNY. DON'T TAKE ISSUE WITH ME IF YOU WANT TO BE MY HONEY.

"What are you smiling about?" Evelyn asked. "If I didn't know better, I'd say you were being mischievous."

"Maybe a teeny tiny bit. But I'd say that I'm having fun. I'm sending Garrison on a scavenger hunt of his own."

"And what's the treasure?" Evelyn asked.

Shirley propped her hands on her hips. "More like *who* is the treasure. That would be me."

"Trust me. He knows how valuable you are. It's been a pleasure to watch the love grow between you two. I believe the bond is always stronger when you start out as friends."

Shirley's phone pinged with a response. It was a string of question marks. She didn't bother to respond, but she was waiting with a smile on her face ten minutes later when he finally rounded the corner and found her standing beside a tree decorated with origami bees made from newspaper.

"Created by none other than the *Charleston Buzz*," Garrison said, shaking his head.

Although the *Charleston Buzz* was now available as an online weekly, there were still people who preferred their copies the old-fashioned way—good ol' black-and-white printed copies. Her mother was one of them. She read it from the first page to the last throughout each week while she sipped her morning coffee or tea.

"I've been in meetings all day, and I still had to put on my thinking cap to find you."

"Was it worth it?"

"Always," Garrison said. He rolled down his shirtsleeves and buttoned them at his wrists. It was late in the workday, and Shirley knew he'd long abandoned his suit jacket. "You're on a roll with solving these clues. Mr. Christmas would be proud."

"Save those words for when I hang the last ornament on the tree and you have the check in hand."

Before they headed to the employee parking lot, Garrison picked up a copy of the *Charleston Buzz* from the news rack positioned near the tree.

"Even though you told me about the loose pooch, it barely looks like anything happened down here."

"Evelyn and Anne took care of it. The two of them work together like a well-oiled machine."

A man rushed by with a phone pressed to his ear. He nearly skidded to a stop in his tracks when he noticed Garrison. "Are you leaving, Mr. Baker? I was hoping to get a few minutes with you before you left."

"No, I'm not leaving, Wayne. You can head up to my office and wait for me if you'd like. I'll be back in a few minutes."

Wayne headed straight to the elevator, apparently to comply with Garrison's suggestion.

"New face?" Shirley asked. "I don't recall seeing him around."

"Wayne is new to the development. He's working with endowments and the like. He's also part of the team working on the proposal for…" Garrison stopped midsentence.

"Let me guess. The funds from the possible contribution. But, hey, no pressure, right?"

"No pressure," Garrison said. "I don't want this to be the only thing we ever talk about." He slowed his pace as if he were hesitant to let their short time together end.

Shirley felt the same way.

When Shirley reached her car, she smelled the unmistakable odor of pipe smoke wafting through the air. She knew that was what she'd noticed the night the boxed poinsettia was left on her front porch. It was the same distinct scent, and it immediately brought back memories of her sitting at her grandfather's feet on the porch while he whittled at wood pieces with a carving knife. Her grandmother would be minding a pot of stew cooking in a cast-iron pot over the woodstove. The thought warmed Shirley's insides.

"Someone has been smoking a pipe," Garrison said.

"You smell it too?" Shirley asked. "Brings back memories."

"For me too," Garrison said.

Shirley appreciated their similar upbringings.

"I wish we could spend time together tomorrow. But I understand that duty calls," Garrison said.

"What about Sunday? You should come over after church for dinner."

"I like the sound of that. What's on the menu?"

Garrison wasn't shy about asking. He loved Shirley's and Mama's cooking and their company. They'd started spending most Sunday afternoons together after leaving worship service at Mother Emanuel. The minute Shirley returned home and let her mother know about their Sunday plans, Mama began planning her meal.

By Saturday morning she had a complete grocery list of all the items Shirley needed to pick up.

"I'm going to have to make a grocery store pit stop sometime today," Shirley said when she walked into Evelyn's home. She scrolled through the notes section on her phone where she'd transferred her mother's written list.

Shirley followed Evelyn around her home as her friend opened blinds, spilling morning sunlight throughout the rooms.

"Mama is going to want to get started on her Sunday meal before this afternoon."

They settled in the living room in the back of the house, where a low fire crackled in the massive fireplace. Shirley joined Evelyn in one of the two high-back wingchairs separated by a nesting table. Atop the table was an open Bible with verses highlighted in pinks and yellows. It was well worn with frayed edges and pages marked with slips of paper and strips of ribbon.

"I have a solution to your grocery store need in a minute," Evelyn said. "But I want to share this verse that I read in my devotion time this morning. I know you've heard it before, but it's always worth reminding ourselves." She picked up her Bible and ran her fingers under the words. "'If any of you lacks wisdom, you should ask God, who gives generously to all without finding fault, and it will be given to you.' That's one of my favorite verses in the book of James." Evelyn marked the page with a ribbon. "God's word applies to every situation. Sometimes we forget it's for everyday living and only think about it when it comes to the big stuff."

"I'd say that imminent donation is big stuff."

"Well, ain't that the truth," Evelyn said, setting her Bible back on the side table. "At any rate, I pray that God gives us wisdom today and that He orders our steps like the Word says in Psalms."

Shirley reached across and squeezed Evelyn's hand. "I agree with you *and* God's word."

Evelyn's husband, James, appeared in the doorway. He was wearing blue flannel pajama pants and a matching robe. He ran the back of his hand along the side of his scraggly, untrimmed beard. Shirley didn't see this side of James often. He was always well groomed with his hair combed neatly. His morning hair was tousled on one side and pressed flat on the other. He didn't seem to mind his appearance. By now they considered each other family.

"Good morning, James," Shirley said. "I hope you don't mind that I'm stealing your wife for the day."

"As long as you return her safely and in one piece," he said with a slow chuckle.

He and Evelyn had celebrated thirty-five years of marriage earlier that year, but it was evident in his eyes that his love hadn't faded—it had endured.

Evelyn pecked her husband on the cheek. "And we better get moving. But first, let's take care of your groceries."

Shirley followed Evelyn upstairs to the study James used as an office. Evelyn sat in the chair behind his desk and asked Shirley for Mama's grocery list. In less than twenty minutes, Evelyn had filled the online cart and chosen a delivery time, and Shirley had paid for the order. The groceries would be delivered at the doorstep before noon.

"I've always wanted to do that but never stopped to try. I didn't realize what I was missing," Shirley said. She was glad she now had one less thing to be concerned with and her focus could be on searching for clues.

"Oh, I do it all the time. It's super convenient and makes things a lot easier for us. I choose a delivery time, and most of the time my groceries are waiting on my doorstep by the time I arrive home from work or shortly thereafter."

"I wish the clues would be waiting for us like that today," Shirley said standing.

"Don't you worry, Shirley. Today is going to be a great day. I have a good feeling about it. The answers are going to come to us this time. Now, bring that clue and let's head out to get the next one."

"I volunteer here with some of my church members a few times a year," Evelyn said as they walked into the sliding double doors of the Caring Hearts and Hands Nursing Center.

The sitting area at the front entrance resembled a quaint living room with two comfortable couches facing each other with a large oak coffee table in between. A collection of magazines was fanned out in the center, and someone had left one open to a recipe for stuffed zucchini. A woman greeted them cordially with a wide smile. Her name tag read PEGGY.

"Welcome to Caring Hearts and Hands. How may I help you?"

"We were hoping to volunteer today," Evelyn said. She signed her name on the sign-in sheet and passed the pen to Shirley.

"Well, we're glad to have you. I assume you're in the database," Peggy said. She picked up the clipboard and began click-clacking her bright red nails across her computer keyboard. "I see that we have Evelyn Perry." She squinted at the screen. "But I don't see Shirley Bashore's name. Have you visited us before?"

"Not in a very long time," Shirley admitted. "So long that I doubt it's in your database." When she thought about it, she probably hadn't been at the nursing center since singing here with her high school chorus.

"I'm afraid all our volunteers have to go through a screening and background check before working with our residents." She handed Shirley a stack of stapled papers. "If you fill these out, we can get you cleared in three to five days."

Three to five days? Shirley didn't have that kind of time.

Shirley began to feel flustered, but she remembered what Evelyn had prayed that morning. God would direct their steps.

"Would it be okay if I waited in this area while Evelyn volunteers with the residents?" Shirley asked.

"I don't think that will be a problem. Make yourself comfortable," Peggy said. "And for you, Evelyn, you're just in time for the morning music class. They need another person to play the triangle since Vita is under the weather. They're practicing for their Christmas program."

"I suppose I can handle that," Evelyn said. "Give me one second and I'll go right back."

Shirley and Evelyn stepped away from the desk to chat in private. "I'm sorry, Shirley. I didn't think about the fact that you'd have to be screened."

"That's why we're a team. No worries. I'll be one step ahead of the game when I'm ready to start volunteering. I've been saying I was going to find a place to serve somewhere in the community ever since I returned to Charleston. And this is perfect."

"I'll discover what I can when I'm back there. I noticed the doors for the administrators' offices are closed. I hope they aren't away for the weekend. Maybe they're roaming around visiting the residents."

Shirley sat while a visitor passed who'd entered carrying two armloads of fluffy folded blankets.

"Enjoy the music class. I can snoop out here while I wait," Shirley said.

"We should ask Peggy if she knows anything. She staffs the front desk and probably sees and hears more than anyone else who works here."

Shirley let Evelyn take the lead with the conversation. Peggy seemed drawn into her words and ignored two incoming calls. Evelyn told her of the clues and ornaments they'd located and how their next clue had led them to Caring Hearts and Hands.

"Oh my," Peggy said. "I haven't heard anything about it, but I wouldn't put it past the people in charge if they didn't tell me a thing. For some reason they find a way to keep all the critical information away from me, and I have no idea why."

Shirley could probably come up with a few ideas.

"Alicia is on duty this weekend. She stepped out briefly, but she should return in about thirty minutes."

When Peggy turned her back, Shirley gave Evelyn a thumbs-up. They started to hear what sounded like a very slow and painful version of "We Wish You a Merry Christmas," and Evelyn hurried down the hallway, following the sign pointing to the resident living areas and the recreation room.

Shirley had barely stepped away from the receptionist desk when she heard Peggy pick up the phone.

"Can you believe it?" Peggy said. "And from what they think, there's probably a clue hidden in one of the resident's rooms."

Evelyn had said no such thing. Shirley didn't bother to listen to the rest of the story Peggy was concocting. She turned her attention to the Christmas tree in the lobby. Tinsel icicles were draped on the ends of the branches. There were also slips of paper hanging here and there using red pieces of ribbon. Shirley started at the top and read every slip of paper—in case Mr. Christmas had decided to veer from the usual. She'd gotten comfortable and assumed the clues would always be delivered in gold envelopes. But what if that wasn't the case?

Shirley squatted to get a closer look at the last slips of paper on the lowest branch. Like most of the others, they were short prayers or Christmas wishes.

"Let's see what dream we can help fulfill," someone said from the other side of the tree. The branches obstructed Shirley's view. It wasn't until she stood and peeped around that she was able to see not only a young woman but a Labrador retriever standing obediently by her side. When the woman patted the side of the dog's head, he lay down and rested his head on top of his paws. He gazed up at Shirley, but he was as still as a statue.

"Someone has trained him well," Shirley said.

The woman bent down and rubbed the dense light brown fur on the dog's side. "Yes. He's a trained and certified therapy pet. We come on Saturdays. They've really fallen in love with King, haven't they, boy?"

Shirley had heard of the benefits of pet therapy and how doing something as simple as holding a guinea pig or petting a cat could stabilize blood pressure or boost moods for patients.

"Can I pet him?" Shirley asked.

"Sure."

She kneeled and rubbed the area behind King's ears. They pricked. "I know the dog's name, but I don't know yours,"

"I'm Kelsey."

"How long have you had King?"

"It will be two years on Christmas," Kelsey said. "I fell in love with him when I attended the Home for the Holidays Adopt a Pet program with a guy who was my boyfriend at the time. A few months later I dumped the boyfriend but kept the dog."

"Based on how lovable King looks, I'd say you made the right choice."

"He's my closest friend. He definitely changed my life."

Kelsey's words made Shirley think of how much Mr. Christmas had loved his dog, Major.

"I've been waiting for you all day," Mr. Christmas said. He was sitting in the chair near the window. "I'd like to go outside."

Shirley smiled at him. "Mr. Christmas, you know any of your nurses could've taken you down."

"I know. But I like our conversations. You've spoiled me," he said. He used Shirley's arm to steady himself, then shuffled over to his wheelchair.

Shirley took her time taking Mr. Christmas downstairs. She could see his whole body relax when she pushed him into the Grove.

"Do you see that dog over there?" Mr. Christmas raised a shaky hand and pointed to beagle being led around on a leash. "He looks like my Major. That dog loved everybody, and he never met a stranger—which didn't make him much of a guard dog at all."

"My mom wanted a dog recently, but I didn't think it was a good idea," Shirley confessed. She positioned Mr. Christmas's wheelchair near one of the benches then sat beside him to enjoy the view of people watching.

"A dog would be an excellent idea for your mother. Us old people like constant companionship."

Maybe he was right, Shirley thought. "I'll give it some consideration."

"Of course you should," Mr. Christmas said. "And if you get a pet, go to the North Charleston Animal Shelter. Tell them I sent you."

"Tell them I sent you," Shirley said aloud.

"Excuse me. Tell who? Tell them what?" Kelsey hugged King around the neck.

"I promise you, I'm not crazy. But I have to go," Shirley said, rushing toward the front door.

"Oh, wait!" Peggy called after her. "Should I give your friend a message?"

"Yes!" Shirley said. She'd been so excited that she'd forgotten about Evelyn. "Can you go back and tell her we need to leave as soon as possible? I'll be waiting in the car."

Chapter Twelve

TEN MINUTES LATER EVELYN SLIPPED into the passenger's seat of Shirley's car.

"Tell me the good news," Evelyn said, expectantly.

"First, Mama's groceries have been delivered. Second, we're headed to the North Charleston Animal Shelter."

"But I didn't even get to speak to the administrator. That's who I was waiting for after we finished the Christmas performance practice."

"Trust me on this. I don't think we need to." Shirley pulled up the address of the animal shelter and set her phone in the mount attached to her windshield. She explained her theory as she pulled out into the street.

"'A loving, caring home is something that's not minor. Take pause and offer a life that could be finer.'" She drummed her thumbs on the steering wheel as she drove. "Something that's not minor—is major. That was the name of Mr. Christmas's beagle that he adopted from the North Charleston Animal Shelter."

"Okay," Evelyn said, listening thoughtfully.

"Take pause. Maybe it's a play on words. He meant paws. P-A-W-S."

"That wisdom we talked about this morning is kicking in," Evelyn said.

"You said the answers would come to us. And they literally did. What you shared with me this morning wasn't just about the clues. It reminded me that God is concerned about the things that concern us."

Shirley tuned the radio to one of the Christian stations that was playing carols twenty-four hours a day until Christmas. Evelyn tried to help Shirley think of a Christmas gift for Garrison, but when they pulled into the parking lot at the animal shelter, she was still at a loss.

"You'll know it when you see it," Evelyn decided.

"I keep saying the same thing, but I hope I see it soon."

Photos of the pets available for adoption were posted in the lobby. The pictures were tacked to a bulletin board that was decorated like a huge gift. Images of the pets that had already found new homes were tacked to a bulletin board decorated like a fireplace.

"It's a wonderful day to take home a new friend. I'm Luna. How can I help you?"

When Luna introduced herself as the director of the animal shelter, Shirley didn't waste any time beating around the bush.

"I'm Shirley Bashore, and Mr. Benjamin Christmas told me to make sure I let you know that he sent me."

Luna's eyes widened like saucers. "I'll be right back." She disappeared down a short hallway and within seconds returned holding the gold envelope and gift box.

"Someone from the Christmas family called me in October. I thought they wanted to talk about pet adoptions, since Mr. Christmas was one of our most committed supporters. I never imagined they'd be calling about one of his last wishes."

Shirley reached for the items, but Luna held them out of her reach. "There's one stipulation before I'm able to give you the items. You have to walk through the dog adoption room."

Luna's expression softened as she spoke. The heart she had for animals was evident, and she probably hoped that with the requirement Mr. Christmas had left behind, Shirley would leave with a furry, four-legged friend.

Not happening, Shirley thought.

They walked down a hallway where Shirley expected to be led to a room that contained kennels or maybe playpens. But each shelter dog waiting for adoption had its own designated area set up like a comfortable living room. There was a chair for interested adopters, a rug, a television, and even an appropriately sized doggy bed.

"We like to call them real-life rooms," Luna said. "It helps the animals prepare to go home with their forever families."

"How neat," Evelyn said.

"They return to the kennels overnight, but in the mornings our volunteers bring them to their living room areas and take time to sit with them. It's a low-stress environment."

The dogs were contained by a door tall enough to keep them from escaping, but low enough for an average adult to see inside.

"Oh, look at him, Shirley." Evelyn cooed at a French bulldog. "He's adorable, and he looks like he's smiling."

According to the information posted on the outside of the door, the dog's name was Chub, and he was four years old. Chub ran to the door in excitement, his backside wiggling with joy.

"Can I go inside?" Evelyn asked Luna.

"Definitely."

"Have fun," Shirley said, amazed at how the first dog Evelyn saw had stolen her heart immediately. Right now, Shirley had a one-track mind. She needed to walk through the corridor of adoption rooms, acquire the next clue, and be on her way. The day was still young, and she wanted to find as many clues and ornaments as possible.

"Well, look at you," Shirley said when she came to a room about halfway down the hallway. "This one took a few laps around Mercy Hospital this week. He left behind quite a mess."

"I heard about that. We're waiting to see if someone comes to claim him. He was hyperactive when he first arrived, but he's calmed down quite a bit. He only goes crazy when it's feeding time."

Shirley didn't know if she believed that.

Luna slowly trailed her, lingering a few steps behind and giving Shirley the heartfelt stories of how each dog had arrived at the shelter.

"The Christmas family adopted their dogs only from here," Luna said. "They even invited me to their doggy reunion, where every member of the Christmas family brought their dog to their gardens in the back of the estate. The female dogs wore English fascinators, and the male dogs wore ascots. It was a sight to see. I believe the Christmas dogs lived a life better than I do." She shook her head.

Shirley laughed at a Chihuahua who ran around in circles at the sight of people. Watching him made Shirley dizzy.

"We named him Chase," Luna explained. "Because he always runs around like he's trying to catch something."

Shirley had finally made it to the end of the corridor. When she looked into the last room, a small pup trotted to the door. Her fur was shiny, and a pink collar was fastened around her neck.

"This is Queen Victoria," Luna said. She curtsied.

Queen Victoria looked at Shirley with inquisitive, bright eyes, but didn't fly into a frenzy like her next-door neighbor. She barked once in greeting, then sat back on her hind legs. Shirley tried to shake the feeling. She really did. It was probably the same thing Evelyn had felt when she and James ended up fostering a miniature dachshund puppy at the beginning of the year. She tried to pull her eyes away, tried to walk off and leave the dog for another loving family. But Shirley knew in a split second that it wasn't going to happen. Mr. Christmas had done it. He had really done it.

She turned the knob and stepped in the living space. The volume of the TV was low, but a video of puppies frolicking in a field of sunflowers was playing, then it cut to another scene with them romping through snow.

"Hello, Queen," Shirley said. The dog stood on all fours and wagged her tail. "Will she let me pick her up?"

"You bet," Luna said. "She has an extremely calm temperament, and she loves to be snuggled."

Shirley gently scooped her up in the fold of her arms and walked with her to the recliner. She settled in the chair with Queen Victoria. She couldn't have been more than a foot tall and maybe ten pounds. She was puppy royalty at its best.

"I hope I'm not about to do something I'll come to regret," Shirley said to Evelyn when her friend joined her.

"Trust me," Evelyn said. "You'll never regret it. Regina is going to be thrilled."

Evelyn rubbed Queen Victoria under her chin, and the dog panted like she knew what was coming next. She jumped out of Shirley's arms and ran to the door, looking back and forth as if to say, *"Come on, let's go home."*

"Are you saying what I think you're saying?" Luna asked.

"Yes."

"Well, there is an interview process, and some people seem to think the questions are a bit invasive. But we want to make sure you and your household are suitable to take on the responsibility of having a dog."

"I'm fine with that," Shirley said.

"And typically there's a fee associated with adopting one of our dogs, but for you, that's already been taken care of. Courtesy of Mr. Christmas, of course."

How did he know?

Luna opened the door and stepped out into the hallway. "If you give me a few minutes, I'll bring you the paperwork and get started with your interview. It looks like Queen Victoria has found a new castle."

"A clue, an ornament, and a queen. Who would have ever thought that would be in the plan today?" Shirley said.

Not only had Mr. Christmas taken care of the adoption fees, but he had also made sure Shirley was equipped with everything she and her mother would need to make Queen Victoria's transition from the shelter to a new home comfortable. She was already trained, so crate training wasn't necessary. Luna had instructed Shirley to back her car up to the rear door of the shelter, and the volunteers had loaded a crate, a food-and-water system that automatically released food on a timer, and some squeaky dog toys.

They'd dropped Queen Victoria at Evelyn's house with James until they returned and until Shirley decided if she wanted to spring the surprise on her mother now or wait until Christmas Day.

They'd called Joy and Anne so they could listen in on the next clue.

"Shirley, I bet she's the cutest thing ever," Joy said. "If you need another doggy sitter, I'm your gal."

Shirley snapped a photo of the ornament that had awaited them at the shelter and sent it to their group text. It was a figurine of Mr. Christmas's beagle, Major, wearing a Santa hat.

"But now back to business," Shirley said. "Let me read the next clue again. 'Now is the time for a journey between two saints. Hushed voices as you go along or there will be complaints.'"

"I believe you should start with the Cathedral of St. John the Baptist," Evelyn suggested.

"But that's only one saint," Joy noted. "The clue said it's a journey between two saints."

"I can explain," Evelyn said.

Evelyn was a history buff and enjoyed recounting the historical facts and accounts of Charleston almost as much as her husband did. If something or someone had its roots in Charleston, then Evelyn probably knew about it.

"The Cathedral of St. John the Baptist sits on the original site of the Cathedral of St. John and St. Finbar, the first Roman Catholic cathedral in Charleston that was constructed in the 1850s. But it was burned down in a fire that ravaged a large part of Charleston in December 1861."

"Was it the same fire that burned down Mercy Hospital all those years ago?" Shirley asked.

"No, but it did happen in the same year during the Civil War. They're not sure of the origin of the Great Charleston Fire of 1861, but it was pushed through the city by a cold front with high winds. The blaze didn't burn itself out until the next day, but by then it had consumed over five hundred and forty acres, almost six hundred homes and businesses, and five churches. One of those churches was the Cathedral of St. John and St. Finbar."

"You're a walking history book on this subject," Joy said.

"I was leafing through the collection in James's study one day and came across a book written about the history of architectural structures in Charleston. I was hooked from there."

Shirley pulled out of the driveway and headed toward Broad Street. She knew the area well. The Cathedral of St. John the Baptist was a massive Gothic structure that towered in the downtown landscape. She remembered visiting as a child, but the clearest memory she recalled was when one of her many crushes asked for half of her turkey sandwich. She readily agreed, then watched in horror as he gave it to another girl who'd forgotten her lunch. Who could listen to a tour guide when your heart had been shattered? When she should have been cherishing her hometown's rich and storied history, she was more concerned with the breakups and makeups happening among her classmates.

Shirley pulled against the curb in front of the cathedral. Though she didn't remember the history without Evelyn's brief lesson, she could still recall its stained glass windows, the marbled altar, and the way the tall arches seemed to point toward heaven.

"Wait right here," Shirley told Evelyn. She jumped out and went to the front entrance and pulled the door, fully expecting to go inside, but it was locked.

Shirley groaned. If the cathedral was closed for the weekend, this would throw them off their timeline to find as many clues that day as possible.

"As you saw, the doors are locked. Maybe if someone is inside they'll come out eventually. We should probably stake out here for a while."

"Or we can call and see if someone answers." Evelyn tapped her phone screen.

"At least there's mass this evening at five," Shirley said. "I wish it was earlier."

"We have four hours. What should we do?"

"What everyone else is doing this time of year. Christmas shopping."

A knock on the window shocked Shirley, and she let out a yelp. She put a hand over her heart, feeling the *thump, thump*. A set of wide eyes behind thick glasses that peered into the window belonged to a man wearing black from head to toe, except for his uncovered, bald head. The sprigs of hair that were combed over the top of his scalp flipped over like a disconnected awning.

Shirley lowered the window enough to hear his voice.

"Are you here to drop off greenery clippings?" he asked, looking from Shirley to the empty back seat. "You can pop the trunk."

"No, sir," Shirley said. She felt comfortable letting the window down halfway. "I don't have any greenery clippings."

"I apologize. I was across the street when I saw you pulling on the doors of the cathedral. We're collecting greenery today to decorate for Christmas."

"I wish we had something to offer. Sorry to disappointment."

"No worries," the man said. His glasses were fogged, and he took them off and wiped them across the front of his jacket. "Is there something I can help you with? Mass isn't until five o'clock."

"Maybe," Evelyn said, leaning forward to see past Shirley. "This is my friend Shirley Bashore, and right now she has one of the biggest assignments in the city. You're going to want to hear about this."

"I'm Timothy. Come on inside."

They sat on the back row of the dark oak pews where Shirley could admire the meticulous beauty of the stained glass windows. The altar seemed miles away, yet still close somehow. It was always a place Shirley was drawn to, a place where she felt nearer to God. Evelyn told Timothy what she knew of the cathedral's history and why they'd come there in search of their next clue.

"You surely know your history," Timothy said. "It took one hundred and three years for us to finish the entire construction of this edifice. The spire and steeple weren't added or consecrated until 2010. I never had the pleasure of knowing Mr. Christmas or his family in a personal way, but I know him by name." He cleared his throat. "Especially by the name on the bottom of the checks. We received two substantial donations over the span of his lifetime, one before I was even born. He even had boxes of greenery delivered to us around this time every year. And as much as I would like to say that we were part of his final act of kindness, I know of nothing. But what I can offer you are my prayers."

"We'll gladly take those too," Shirley said, meaning it.

"Now if you'll excuse me, ladies." He stood up and threw his coat over his arm. "I need to get back to collecting greenery."

Shirley tapped her fingers on the back of the pew in front of her. Her mind mulled the clue. *A journey between two saints.* Two saints. St. Nicholas? Two St. Nicks. Should they be looking for two men with rosy cheeks and white beards? They'd already looked around Charleston for Santa Claus when they were searching for the second clue.

"You're not calling it quits for the day, are you, Shirley? I think we should return at five o'clock for mass. There could be someone watching and waiting for your arrival here."

"I'm not giving up," Shirley assured her.

"We have the rest of the day to figure it out," Evelyn said. She swiped across her phone and held it up for Shirley. "As you can see, Queen Victoria is being thoroughly entertained and cared for." James had texted a photo of Queen Victoria holding a snowman squeezy toy in her mouth. James's face was smushed against her fur, and he was wearing reindeer antlers.

"My husband's students and colleagues think he's always serious. If they only knew."

"What's your secret to lifelong love and a committed marriage?" Shirley asked as they descended the cathedral steps and headed for her car.

"I can tell you what's worked for us, although I think each couple has to find the things that make their marriage work," Evelyn said. "James and I have a mutual respect for each other. That helps squash unnecessary arguments and offenses. Over the years I've tried to see James as God sees him. Neither of us will ever be perfect, but God is always working to make us better. Individually and together. You and Garrison will work together to create the life you'll love."

Shirley slowed as she approached the car. She looked around, not sure who or what she was looking for. The hair on the back of her neck stood up even though the only people around were passing by in cars.

"Do you smell that?" Shirley asked Evelyn. "It's faint, but I smell pipe smoke. It's like walking past someone who wasn't smoking at the moment, but the odor has soaked into the threads of their clothes."

Evelyn frowned. "I can't say that I do. I can't smell a thing. But what I can do is hear Christmas caroling coming from that direction. We didn't wear these walking shoes for nothing. We can help the time pass quickly and see what's going on while we wait to come back for mass."

"I'm right behind you, Evelyn," Shirley said. "Where there are carolers, there is Christmas and maybe two saints. Perhaps a jolly old Saint Nicholas or two. It's a stretch, but I'm kind of grasping at straws here."

Shirley zipped her jacket and pulled the hood over her head. Even in her forties, she could hear her mother's scolding voice when she tried to leave the house without being properly clothed when the weather called for it. *"I don't care how it feels outside, it's still winter. You need to wear a coat and cover your head."*

The downtown area of Charleston was alive with holiday charm. Lights twinkled on every lamppost and around the windows of every building and storefront shop. Horses pulled carriages full of people down cobblestone streets. On the evening after Thanksgiving, she and Garrison had attended the Christmas tree lighting. The multicolored lights on the tall fir were synced to Christmas music for an amazing dancing light display. Afterward, they'd climbed aboard one of the carriages and were served cocoa with marshmallows.

"Would you look at that," Evelyn said as they approached Marion Square, a block of green space between Meeting and King Streets. "That must be a recent addition, because it wasn't here a few days ago."

During the summertime, the students of the College of Charleston claimed the green space area for sunbathing, and Shirley had started to shop the seasonal farmer's market for fresh fruits and vegetables when they set up the space. But currently someone had erected Santa's Village, complete with life-sized greeting cards that had been designed by local high school art students, and roasting pits where a group had gathered to toast s'mores.

"Evelyn, do you see what I see? Two Saint Nicks." Shirley pointed at the old-fashioned carousel, large enough to allow three riders to take a spin. Standing in booths on either side of the entrance were two teenagers dressed like Santa Claus, though not in the typical way. In the place of a furry red suit, they wore red hooded sweatshirts that looked like a Santa suit, including a black belt with a gold buckle printed at the hem of the shirt.

Shirley rushed over. "Hi, I'm Shirley Bashore. Will I receive something if I ride this carousel?"

"You most certainly will," one of the teens said. "Climb aboard, young lady." Shirley found that to be hilarious, since she was obviously at least thirty years his senior.

"I'll enjoy the ride from here," Evelyn said, when she finally caught up with Shirley.

The other young St. Nick flipped a switch, and the carousel came alive with music. Shirley held on to the gold pole that stretched from the top of the tented carousel and down through the body of a white horse wearing a red plume feather on his head and with a painted green and blue saddle.

When the carousel slowed to a stop, Shirley stepped off and steadied her feet. She returned to the teen who had promised to deliver her next clue. He stooped behind the booth out of Shirley's view but popped back up within seconds.

"Here you go, young lady," he said. "A gift for you."

Shirley stared at the candy cane in his hand. He wasn't serious. He *couldn't* be serious. She didn't have time for his youthful sense of humor. He didn't realize how serious it was for her to get the next envelope and clue—and to get it now.

She finally found her words. "A candy cane? Young man, if you're playing jokes, now is not the time."

"I'm sorry, ma'am. We offer candy canes to everyone who rides the carousel. They're for the young and the young at heart." He bent down for another and offered it to Evelyn, who had joined Shirley at her side.

Evelyn slid them out of his hands. "Candy canes are one of my favorites."

"And what about a gold envelope or gold box? Did your boss leave anything like that?"

The other kid spoke up. He pushed the Santa hoodie off his head, revealing a headful of curly black hair that hadn't seen clippers in some time.

"We're working for my dad. He's never given us anything else. We were told to give out these candy canes until we ran out. I promise."

Shirley sighed. "I enjoyed the ride. Merry Christmas."

They chimed "Merry Christmas" together, then retreated to their respective booths. Shirley looked back. They'd probably get a laugh talking about the "crazy lady" later.

"The day is yet young." Evelyn had been encouraging all morning.

"Maybe it's not meant to be to find more than one clue today," Shirley said. "I feel bad about keeping you away from James all day. And I should probably get home and help Mama cook dinner for tomorrow."

"Nonsense," Evelyn said, stopping in front of the roasting pits. "James is fine, especially since we left Queen Victoria there to keep him company. And as for your mother, I've eaten her food before. She knows her way around the kitchen better than the both of us. And didn't you say Dot was coming to keep her company?"

"Yes."

"Then she'll be fine."

"We do still need to return for mass. God works in mysterious ways," Shirley said.

"So does Mr. Christmas." Shirley pulled the folded clue from her jacket pocket.

"'Now is the time for a journey between two saints. Hushed voices as you go along or there will be complaints.'" She frowned. "I got ahead of myself when I ran to the carousel. The rest of the clue didn't fit. Hushed voices. A carousel is not the place for hushed voices."

"Excuse me, ladies."

They were approached by a tall, slender man who carried a limp, sleeping child on his shoulder. The woman beside him pushed a stroller that was piled high and stuffed with shopping bags.

"Can you point us in the right direction to get to the Gateway Walk?" he asked with no interest in his voice.

Shirley presumed the woman with him was his wife. Her hair was twisted in a messy bun, and her hair's stray strands were held in place with a wide headband. She looked disheveled to say the least.

"We're visiting from Virginia, and it's on my list of top ten things to see on a Charleston walking tour. I think I might've been too ambitious today and also slightly sidetracked." Her eyes went to the bounty of her shopping spree. She looked up at her husband with hopeful eyes. "What do you say we rest a bit, enjoy some s'mores, and then keep going?"

He bent down and kissed her on the forehead, an act of silent agreement.

"I'll get you back on track for the Gateway Walk. It's easy to do," Evelyn said. She used the woman's brochure to map out their route with her finger. "You're right around the corner. The walk starts at the gates of the St. John's Lutheran Church on Archdale Street and ends at St. Philip's Episcopal Church."

"Evelyn! You got it." Shirley grabbed her friend's arms and jumped up and down. "Have a nice stroll through Gateway Walk, but we have to run now."

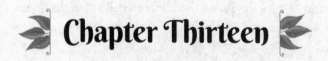

Chapter Thirteen

IT ALL MADE SENSE NOW. The journey between two saints meant the walkway between the two churches, St. John's Lutheran Church and St. Philip's Episcopal Church. Ten pairs of wrought iron gates were positioned along the course that mazed throughout the city. It was a known tourist attraction, but even Charleston residents regularly enjoyed the trailway. Shirley had always felt like it was a secret backyard to the city with its gardens, graveyards, and fern-lined walkways. On both her and Cynthia's tenth birthdays, her father had her mother dress them up in their fanciest church clothes, and he brought his Polaroid camera and took a photo at every wrought iron gate. Shirley remembered her excitement as the instant camera spit out each photograph. She'd fan it through the air until the chemicals spread across the film and the photograph magically appeared.

Shirley slowed her gait when she realized Evelyn wasn't keeping up.

"You said I got it," Evelyn said. "What did I get?"

Shirley explained all the thoughts swirling around in her head. "The Charleston Library Society is located inside the Gateway Walk between the gates at St. John's Lutheran Church and St. Philip's Episcopal Church. And you have to have hushed voices at the library or you're bound to get complaints." Shirley snapped her fingers. "And you know what else? Mr. Christmas donated several sets of rare and historic books to the library's collection. I remember the day he told me about it."

Mr. Christmas waved Shirley into the room. She'd opened the door slowly when she heard another voice in the room but found it to be someone reading by his bedside. Shirley slipped quietly into a chair in the corner while the woman read in a steady, melodic voice. After about ten minutes, she slipped a bookmark between the pages and closed the cover of the hardbound book.

"This is my great-great-niece," Mr. Christmas said, introducing the young woman. "She comes to read to me every now and then. I used to enjoy reading historical books, memories, and the classics, but she's gotten me hooked on whodunits, believe it or not."

"I think that's wonderful," Shirley said.

"Much better than my other nephew, who sent me a book over here about aging well." He pushed the incline button on the rail of his bed then adjusted the cannula in his nose, which was connected to the oxygen machine. "I think I've done about all of the aging I'm going to do."

"And you've done it well," Shirley said.

His niece kissed his forehead, which was covered in age spots, then slipped her smooth hand into his wrinkled one. "Love you, Uncle Benny. I'll see you next Thursday at the same time."

"Did you see to the rest of the collection?"

"*Yes. The estate manager made sure everything was boxed properly and arranged for them to be transported to the collection at the Charleston Library Society. I'll follow through to make sure it arrives.*"

"*That's my girl,*" he said. "*My fellow bibliophile. And did you take out the ones that you wanted for your personal collection?*"

"*I did that first,*" she said. She reached into a rolling crate and pulled out leather-bound journals. She stacked them in towers beside the nightstand.

"*They are probably the most valuable books in my entire collection, but they are never to leave the Christmas family. Every person of every generation should have access to my journals.*" He lifted one with green leather and gold leaf trim along the edges of the pages. "*This is the story of my life from the time when I was in my thirties. Not everything but a good part of it.*"

"*Priceless,*" Shirley said.

"*It says in the book of James that life is like a vapor that appears for a while then vanishes away. I think only the old realize that it's true.*" Mr. Christmas picked up a cup of water with a trembling hand. Shirley helped to steady it so he could drink until his thirst was satisfied.

"*Get busy living.*"

Shirley and Evelyn ascended the gray marble steps that led to the arched entryway of the Charleston Library Society. Red velvet bows hung from the black sconces positioned on both sides of the glass double doors. Shirley pulled open the door, and they stepped into the quiet warmth of the library. The building was as grand inside as it was outside, with a black-and-white checkered floor and tall windows. Oil paintings of men Shirley couldn't readily identify hung on the walls, their eyes following Shirley as she walked by. Other than that, there wasn't a person in sight.

"It doesn't look like they get much action on Saturdays," Shirley said.

A woman in a plaid A-line skirt appeared from around a tall bookshelf. "Good afternoon."

"Good afternoon. We'd like to see the collection donated by Mr. Benjamin Christmas, if possible. Could you tell us where we can find it?"

"Are you members of the Society? We're only open for members on Saturdays and Sundays."

Shirley fished around in her purse for her membership card, which she thankfully found in her billfold. It was almost expired, but good enough for today's entrance. Evelyn showed her card also.

The woman tapped her finger on her watch. "It's almost time for us to close. We're closing earlier than usual today because we're having our staff Christmas party." She beckoned them to follow her. "The Christmas collection is housed downstairs in one of our private rooms. The employee who usually handles our special collections isn't here today, but I'm willing to make an exception." She looked at Evelyn. "I believe we've met briefly, although it's been some time ago. Your husband is a history professor at College of Charleston, correct?"

"He is."

"I've attended several of his presentations over the last few years. I'm sure you can handle the collections properly."

"Thank you," Evelyn said. "And I will."

"My mother always said working hard and having a good reputation will open doors for you," Shirley said. "Thanks to James."

"Don't let anyone know about this favor, if you wouldn't mind. I usually follow the rules."

"Your secret is safe with us," Evelyn said. "Hopefully we'll be in and out fairly quickly."

They shed their coats when they were led to a private reading room.

"The collection is housed behind these glassed-in bookcases," she said, using a key to unlock them. "If I don't make it back down before you leave, I'll lock the doors when I return on Monday."

"We appreciate you—" Shirley paused.

"Libby."

"We appreciate you, Libby."

Libby left the room quietly, as if she walked on clouds. As soon as she closed the door, Shirley looked at the rows of hardback books. Their original covers were slightly faded but mostly in impeccable condition. She began at the top shelf and ran her fingers along the outward facing spines. The collection was exhaustive, and Shirley laid eyes on each one over the next ten minutes. The hairs on the back of her neck stood up as she stopped on one titled *The Christmas Miracle*.

"This is the one." Shirley didn't know why she whispered to Evelyn when it was obvious they were the only two in the room.

Shirley slid the heavy volume from the shelf, using two hands to lift and balance the book. Nestled behind it was the gold box. Evelyn reached in for the ornament as Shirley set the spine of the book down on the oak table with a loud, echoing thud. She pulled back the cover, and the pages opened naturally where the gold envelope was buried within the creases.

"We've struck gold, pun intended," Shirley said, waving the envelope in the air. She wanted to whoop for joy, but she contained herself. She'd been careful with opening the other envelopes, but she ripped into this one in her excitement. "Wait, we should check out the ornament first, and you should do the honor, Evelyn. If it wasn't for you being by my side and for James being the man that he is, none of this would've happened today."

Evelyn lifted the top of the box, looped her finger through the red ribbon at the top, and lifted out an ornament shaped like a stack of books. The titles of Christmas classics were printed on the spines.

"'Twas the Night Before Christmas' is one of my favorites," Evelyn said.

Shirley thought about her father's fun habit of rearranging and rewriting things like nursery rhymes and the prose of popular books to fit their family. She had fond memories of their bedtime readings when she and her sister, Cynthia, would be the main characters in fairy tales like "Little Red Riding Hood." At Christmastime, his reimagination of "'Twas the Night Before Christmas" was a family favorite.

"'Twas the Night Before Christmas and all through the Mercy halls…" Shirley stopped and thought before continuing. "We were looking for clues both great and small. The patients were nestled all snug in their beds, but the nurses still knew there was a busy night ahead. Shirley and her friends needed to find the next clue. They had to make haste. There was so much to do."

Click. Darkness. *Click.* Darkness.

Suddenly, the lights began to turn off around them. Had it not been for the nearly ceiling-height windows, they would have been stranded in darkness.

"That's our cue to get going," Evelyn said. "Either they thought we'd already gone, or Libby the Librarian forgot we were down here."

Shirley slid the book back in place and grabbed her coat. If they hurried, they might be able to work on one more clue. The sooner they got moving in the remaining daylight, the better.

Shirley heard the slam of the door and without question knew it wasn't good.

"Are you thinking what I'm thinking?" Shirley asked Evelyn.

"I am, Shirley. We're locked in."

They rushed to the window to see if they could catch a glimpse of someone—anyone—they could alert to their situation. Walking down a nearby pathway, ears covered in large headphones, was a custodian. Shirley had seen the middle-aged man earlier when he'd come through to empty papers in a nearby trash can. He had been wearing the same headphones then, humming quietly as he swiped a cloth across the tops of the bookshelves. He'd nodded his head at them in acknowledgment but kept busily along his way.

Shirley rapped on the window to try and get his attention, but to no avail. Evelyn joined her chorus of knocks on the window, but he didn't even to stop to turn his head.

"He'll never hear us with those things covering his ears," Shirley said. "Let's check all the doors, including the front door. A lot of times they're locked from the outside but able to be opened from the inside."

Shirley pulled on the handle of the front door. Nothing. She jiggled it again to make sure. Locked. Typically someone would be passing by on the sidewalk, but the only thing remotely nearby were three birds, jumping around and pecking at the cement. She banged on the door and caught the attention of a squirrel skittering by. He turned his head toward Shirley, staring at her with round black eyes.

"If only you could help me," Shirley said. She turned back to go find Evelyn.

"No luck for you either?" Evelyn asked, looking frustrated.

Shirley felt bad for dragging her friend around all morning and afternoon, and now she had to take responsibility for this predicament as well. She shoved her hands in the deep pockets of her coat. "We'll call someone. Sooner or later we'll get out of here."

Shirley tried to stay calm, but evidently the panic showed on her face. She pushed her hands in and out of her coat pockets, then shoved them into the pockets sewn into the lining in the off chance she'd slipped it there.

"You don't have your phone, do you?" Evelyn asked.

"It seems I've lost it. Again." She blew out a long, frustrated sigh. "We'll use yours."

"That would work if I hadn't left it in your glove compartment. I put my wallet in my coat pocket and left everything else in your car."

"Then we'll use the library phone. Maybe there's a list posted of the employees. We usually keep an emergency list posted somewhere at our nurses' stations. We'll call someone to come back and let us out."

"Good idea," Evelyn said, trailing her like a shadow.

Shirley walked behind the circulation desk, and she immediately felt like she was intruding on someone's personal space. It didn't feel right to meddle around in a private work area. She was careful not to touch anything, except for when she picked up the phone. There was no dial tone. How was there no dial tone? She pushed nine to try and get an outside line. The phone was dead.

She looked at the sticky notes and index cards tacked around the area. There was a reminder about a ten o'clock dentist appointment for the upcoming Wednesday, a note to take more ornaments to the society's Christmas tree at Mercy, and a reminder to purchase stamps. The only list of numbers she noticed was for in-house extensions.

"What are we going to do?" Evelyn asked.

Shirley looked around. "We can always read to pass the time away." Shirley needed to find the humor in their situation. "But seriously, I need to retrace my steps and look for my phone while we still have a decent amount of light."

She paced slowly up and down each aisle. Shirley knew after the first time that they would never find it. It wasn't a needle in a haystack. A phone could be easily spotted.

"When is the last time you remember having it?" Evelyn asked her once they'd walked the area several times.

It took a moment for Shirley to recall. "I took a selfie on the carousel and texted it to Garrison. It must have fallen out of my pocket somewhere in the area." She shrugged. "And here we are."

"Let's look at the bright side of things," Evelyn said. "We're warm and we're safe, although I'm not sure what they will think when they see your car abandoned in front of the church. I'm sure James and Garrison will eventually come looking for us."

"I don't think they'll have to," Shirley said, when she spotted the figures lurking on the side of the building near the windows.

Chapter Fourteen

"WITH ALL THE WALKING AROUND we'd been doing, we set off the silent alarm," Shirley said to Dot. "Even though the police arrived, it took a while before they were able to contact someone who could return to unlock the building."

"That was quite an adventure," Dot said. "I don't blame you for calling it a day after that. Solving two clues in one day is impressive."

"And I'm very proud of her," Garrison said. He walked into the living room with another glass full of sweet tea. At his request, her mother had brewed a pitcher that morning before leaving for church because, as he'd said, "A soul food meal isn't complete without sweet tea."

"I was worried when you weren't calling me back," her mother said. She'd settled in her favorite chair and had a throw draped over her legs. "I settled down a little when Garrison told me you were probably busy running around the city."

"That and being careless. My phone was exactly where I thought it would be. Someone had turned it in to one of the boys manning the carousel booth."

Her mother rubbed her knees. Shirley would have to remember to massage them with ointment before bed.

"Tell us about the ornaments. What did you get at the animal shelter and library?"

She'd definitely gotten more than a clue and an ornament at the animal shelter and it took everything Shirley had not to spill the beans. When she'd arrived back at Evelyn's house, Queen Victoria had trotted up to Shirley and weaved through her legs until Shirley picked her up and scratched her crown. She was sure Mama's lap would be one of her favorite places. If Queen Victoria was hoping for a home where she'd be spoiled, she was coming to the right place.

"I'll do better than tell you, I'll show you."

Shirley went to her bedroom and returned with the two gold boxes.

As a retired librarian, Dot immediately proclaimed that the ornament shaped like the stack of books was her favorite.

"They have such remarkable details."

"And this one is Mr. Christmas's dog, Major."

"He looks real. I wouldn't be surprised if he barked," her mother said. She stared at it for a moment—almost longingly—before she set the ornament back in the gold box. "Now what did the next clue say?"

It was what everyone else wanted to know but was too afraid to ask.

"Come on," her mother urged. "Spill the beans. We're curious."

She knew the rules. Everyone had been told of the implications and the consequences if they dared cross the line.

Shirley went back to her bedroom again and reemerged with the hastily torn envelope. All eyes were on her, like she was the next to last person standing for the school spelling bee.

"We're not going to say a word," Mama promised. "I heard the rules with my own ears. You can't get direct help, which we won't give. If you can't trust your family, who can you trust?"

Shirley pulled out the clue and read it before she changed her mind. "'Through five generations it was never lost, though it traveled over the oceans. Visitors take them home, but we leave them here. It's sweet history in motion.'"

It was slight. It was quick. Yet Shirley noticed it anyway. A knowing glance had passed between her mother and Dot.

"Interesting," Garrison said. He rubbed the hair on the end of his chin. It had become grayer in the last few months, and Shirley was fond of the salt-and-pepper look.

Both her mother and Dot avoided her gaze, confirming her suspicions. They knew the answer to the clue. One look at Garrison and Shirley realized that he'd surmised the same thing. He'd been around the duo enough to be able to interpret their silence, their unspoken words, and the way they communicated with squinted eyes or raised brows.

"And they didn't utter a word?" Joy asked the next day when they'd gathered in the conference room on the administrative floor.

"They couldn't, and honestly I didn't want them to. We're starting at square one like we've always done."

Evelyn had secured the room so they could have the space they needed to review the items for the holiday market, which was set to start in two days, and to hold a short meeting with the vendors, who were set to begin arriving at any minute.

Aurora's constant badgering was weighing on everyone. She wanted to turn everything into a major production when Anne had decided that in this case simplicity was best.

Aurora wanted each department to have a designated time to shop, but Anne overruled it and said the employees should shop at their own discretion. Aurora pushed for customized placards for each business, but Anne insisted each business could provide their own signage because they typically had their own marketing and branding materials anyway. Aurora wanted carolers to sing at the beginning and ending of each shift since it would be the busiest shopping hours, but Anne decided to use the playlist that Evelyn's niece had set up for her.

Shirley had missed most of the tug-of-war between Anne and Aurora since her attention was being pulled in many different directions.

Twenty-five chairs were set out for the morning's vendor meeting for the holiday market, and before the start of the meeting each of them was filled.

"I'd say we had a perfect turnout." Evelyn noted that there was no empty seat before she passed out an overview to each representative in attendance. She hadn't known what to expect since they'd had to plan a midmorning meeting, but it was the only time they could accommodate all their schedules.

"If anyone would like to grab a snack before we begin, there's fresh fruit, bagels, and beverages in the back," Shirley said. She would wait until the meeting was over and hopefully be able to grab a bite before she had to head back to the cardiac unit.

People seemed reluctant to be the first in line, but once an eager lady jumped up and made her way to the table, others trickled behind her.

"It's no use letting all of this go to waste," she said, putting a bagel, cream cheese, a cluster of grapes, and strawberries on her plate. She wore denim overalls with a red-and-white-striped shirt underneath that matched her socks. The woman was a walking candy cane. And not only that, she was a Chatty Cathy. She made her way around the room, speaking to others and handing out round business cards that were shaped like a piece of wrapped bubble gum.

"She's a spunky one," Joy said. "I bet she's the life of the party wherever she goes."

"Which vendor is she?" Shirley asked. She picked up the business directory Evelyn had printed that contained the business names, contact information, websites, and social media information. She ran her finger along the list. "She looks fun. I bet she owns the toy store, or maybe she's one of the food vendors. We have three, and one of them sells baked goods and homemade candies."

"I guess we'll find out when we do the introductions," Anne said. "She might even be from the bookstore."

But Chatty Cathy wasn't from the bookstore or the toy store, nor was she one of the *invited* food vendors.

"My name is Lyla Poppy," she excitedly announced as the introductions made their way around the room. "I'm the owner of Poppy's Sweet Shoppe, a boutique bakery with the tastiest goodies you'll ever eat. If you ever try my specialty cupcakes, you'll never eat another."

"That's her," Shirley whispered to Joy. "It's *the* Lyla Poppy who called to try and get us to change our mind when she wasn't chosen for the tree festival and again when we couldn't fit her in the holiday market. Both Evelyn and Anne have talked to her to no avail. I guess she's willing to do anything to participate, even invite herself to our meeting."

Joy put her hand on Shirley's arm and led her farther to the back of the room. "But how did she find out the information about our meeting?"

"I have no idea. But she's here, and she doesn't need to be," Shirley said.

"What do we do?"

"We'll have to get her out. As quickly and as quietly as possible so the meeting can continue without interruption," Shirley said.

Lyla was still giving her introduction in full animation. Most of the businesses before had given an abridged description of their business, but Lyla sounded like she planned to give her entire life's history. Although people were looking at each other with raised eyebrows, Lyla didn't seem to notice. And if she did, she didn't seem to care.

Shirley got the attention of Evelyn, who was standing in the front of the room behind Lyla. Shirley swirled her finger in the air, signaling Evelyn to wrap up Lyla's spiel. Evelyn immediately got the point. She also knew by the look on Evelyn's face that she knew Lyla wasn't where she was supposed to be.

"Thank you so much, Ms. Poppy," Evelyn said, coaxing her to the left and closer to the door where Shirley was waiting for her.

"Ms. Poppy, if you could step this way," Shirley said.

"Lyla is fine," she said. "No need to be formal."

"Well, Lyla, we wanted to let you know that we're aware that your name isn't on the list to participate in the holiday market. We appreciate your enthusiasm, but we can't accommodate you this year. There's always next year though."

Lyla shoved her hands in her pockets. "But there are twenty-five businesses participating, and twenty-five chairs in there. If I was in one of those seats, then that means one of the businesses didn't show up. That always happens for events like these, which is why I'm here to take their place."

Shirley looked around for backup, but Joy, Evelyn, and Anne were preoccupied with the meeting. "It doesn't work like that," Shirley said, kind but stern. At least she hoped so. "I'm going to have to ask you to leave, but we keep all the applications for future opportunities."

"I was hoping I wouldn't get this response, but persistence isn't always rewarded," Lyla said. She crossed her arms. If she were a balloon, she would have burst. "There should probably be more people on the committee making these decisions."

"Maybe another year," Shirley said between clenched teeth. She went back into the conference room and closed the door, leaving Lyla behind to stew alone.

"Is she gone?" Joy whispered as she walked by.

"Let's hope so," Shirley said.

The rest of the meeting went off without a hitch. Shirley was relieved that the holiday market was about to be another successful Mercy Christmas event.

"And we have these," Anne said when the ladies were cleaning up. "Lyla Poppy left them behind for us. Apparently, she had other samples as well, but she was insistent that we get this particular batch." Anne pushed a plastic covered tray of assorted cupcakes toward Shirley. "You should reward yourself for a job well done so far."

Each sample tray included a red velvet, pink lemonade, and key lime flavor. According to the handwritten note attached to the top of one of the trays, the cupcakes were both an apology and a bribe. An apology for barging into their meeting uninvited. A bribe to be included in the holiday marketing in case there actually was a last-minute cancellation.

"They almost look too pretty to eat," Shirley said. "I'll save mine for after dinner. I'll reward myself once I return home *after* solving this clue."

Anne slid into the seat beside her and swiveled around to see her. "You said you've been brainstorming about it. What do you have on your list?"

Shirley opened the notebook where she'd jotted down ideas and doodles. "I wrote names of things that travel across oceans. Seashells, ships, sea animals, and seagulls."

"Read the clue one more time, please."

Shirley cleared her throat. "'Through five generations it was never lost, though it traveled over the oceans. Visitors take them home, but we leave them here. It's sweet history in motion.'"

"What about waves or currents?" Anne suggested thoughtfully.

"Hurricanes," Joy added. "We know about those."

"Dreams," Anne said. "Whenever Lili was stationed overseas, she'd always tell Addie that she was going to send her sweet dreams over the ocean."

Shirley wrote as quickly as she could. "That's great, Anne. I was thinking more literal, but maybe that's not what it is." She circled the word *dream* and drew stars beside it. She had to dig deeper. The answer wasn't on the surface. "It may be the only thing on this list that fits the part of the clue that says, 'Through five generations it was never lost.'" She drew a line through the other words on the page.

"Less literal, more figurative."

Evelyn pulled out the pen that had been stuck in her hair and fiddled with it between her fingers. "When I was growing up, my grandpa—I called him Pop-Pop—would tell me these intriguing stories about immigrants in my family. Stories travel across the oceans, and they're passed down so they don't get lost. Storytelling is history in motion."

"I like that too," Shirley said. She added it to her list and drew more stars. "I guess storytelling can also apply to the part about visitors taking them home. Tourists leave knowing our rich history in Charleston, but the stories always stay here with us."

"That's a good thought, Shirley," Evelyn said.

Shirley stood and reached for her belongings. "I'm not sure where I can capture dreams, but I know where I can track down storytellers. Anyone want to come along after work?"

"As long as everything is as it needs to be at the gift shop this afternoon, I'll be happy to join you. But promise me we won't get locked up in any buildings."

"I can't make those promises, Joy." Shirley laughed.

Several hours later Shirley pulled into the driveway of a house painted the color of fading fall grass. It was topped with a brown shingled roof, and the rustic pine door under the portico bore a WELCOME sign that partially obstructed the glass windowpanes.

"So this is the place?" Joy asked as she unbuckled her seat belt.

"We came here years ago as part of one of our family reunion activities. It's a hidden treasure organized by Corrine Watson, one of the members of Mother Emanuel. She can tell a story in a way that makes it come alive. When she talks about Gullah culture I can hear the soul-stirring songs of my ancestors. When she described the spices in okra soup, I could taste the dance of the seasonings on my tongue. She trained other storytellers to carry on the tradition so it wouldn't become a lost art."

Corrine must have heard—or sensed—their arrival. When she looked out the window, Shirley saw the unmistakable crown of white locks that Corrine always wore fashioned into a perfect donut-shaped bun on her head. Her Kente cloth shawl draped her thin frame and covered most of the black knit outfit she wore. The long flowy fabric moved around her ankles like ocean waves at nighttime.

"Shirley Bashore." She opened a door with a smile as bright at the bold yellow jewelry that dangled from her ears and circled her neck. "It's such a pleasure seeing you here. And you brought company."

"Yes ma'am, I did. This is Joy."

"Oh, I love that name, especially at this time of year."

"And I love what you've done in here," Joy said, obviously admiring the bright, culturally inspired decor.

"Thank you," Corrine said. "Please have a seat, ladies." She invited them into a circle of rocking chairs with a soft cushion tied to the seat of each chair.

Shirley looked around. The walls were painted a muted gold hue with enough sheen to highlight the photo gallery on one of the walls. The frames were different styles but matched the pine color of the door. A fire crackled in the fireplace, and there were also scented candles placed strategically on the floor in front of it.

"I knew someone special would be here tonight," Corrine said. "I've had very few guests in the last week, but when God gives me something to do, I do it to the best of my ability and with all of my passion. He has trusted me to tell the stories. This month I've been sharing the stories of Christmas past."

Christmas past. The twinkle in Corrine's eyes. It was her way of letting Shirley know she was in the right place, but Shirley figured she'd need to listen to the story to complete the assignment.

Shirley looked at Joy, who had reached into a nearby basket for a crocheted afghan and was draping it across her legs. Joy winked at her.

"It was the sound of freedom," Corrine began. "Agnes, though tiny and young as she was, had a voice that floated over the night sky. It weaved around the fields and praise houses. She had her mother's voice, her daddy would always say when someone commented on its richness. A mother who'd only held her briefly before her spirit floated away. It was said that Agnes stopped crying at the very moment God called her mother's soul to heaven. Instead, she cooed. She was a happy baby, and her voice brought others comfort at the end of a long working day.

"Christmas was the best time of year for Agnes. It was one of the few times when they enjoyed a handful of days to themselves. While their festivities may not have been as grand with presents and tables full of food, Agnes and her father shared in special moments. He'd used wood scraps to whittle a doll, stained it with rich brown soil from the earth, and wrapped it in a dress made from burlap."

Shirley and Joy were captivated as Corrine told the adventurous story of Agnes, her doll, Mattie, and the Christmas miracles that followed them.

"I could listen to you all night," Shirley said.

"Where did you learn your storytelling skills?" Joy asked.

"I'm like Agnes," Corrine said. "It was a gift from my mother. And to her, from her mother. Four generations of storytelling women."

Four? If Shirley remembered correctly, the clue said five generations. Corrine had made an honest mistake.

"Five generations?" Shirley asked gently, in an attempt to correct her but still with respect for her elder.

"No, it's four generations. I'm sure of it. I'm the fourth generation from my mother's lineage. It began with my great-grandmother, Louisa Mae."

"And who will carry on after you?" Joy asked her.

Corrine's eyes turned down at the corners. "I started this mission with hopes that others with the storytelling gift would raise their voices and ensure that our history never dies. Unfortunately, my three sons don't show any interest in it."

"If those who walk along with you are anywhere near as masterful as you are, then your legacy is surely in good hands."

Corinne clasped her hands at her heart and bowed slightly. She then stood up and looked around as if she'd heard something. She held her hands out in front of her, like she wanted to stop

Shirley and Joy from leaving. "Please wait here. I have something to give you."

After Corinne had left the room, Shirley's stomach growled. "Cupcake, here I come," Shirley said. "I'm going to eat dinner, reward myself with a treat, and watch mindless television for the rest of the night."

"What do you think the ornament will be this time?" Joy asked, folding the afghan and replacing it back among the others.

"That's a good question," Shirley said. "Maybe it's a version of the Mattie doll. Or maybe it's a—"

"Here you go. A special gift from me to you to symbolize and honor one of Charleston's long-standing Gullah traditions." Corinne reached out for Shirley's hand, then slid a bracelet on her wrist. She repeated the same act with Joy.

"It's beautiful." Shirley beamed, genuinely loving the bracelet. But it wasn't what she expected. "Corrine, did you receive anything else that you were directed to give to me specifically?"

"Nothing at all. These gifts were donations. If you don't like it, maybe you can pick something else that you'd prefer, although I don't know what that would be." She bit her lip and looked around the room.

"Oh no, no, no. I'm grateful, and I thank you from the bottom of my heart for your time and for the bracelet. Our visit here was the perfect ending to my day."

"It most definitely was," Joy said. "I'd love to have the contact information for the people who provided the bracelets. I'd like to add them to the jewelry display cases in the hospital's gift shop. I've been making more of an effort to support our local artisans."

"I'm sure they would love that." Corinne gave Joy a business card from a stack on a nearby console table. "They've recently started making these bracelets made of sweetgrass, but they specialize in the sweetgrass baskets. You can't visit Charleston and leave without one as a souvenir."

Before she realized it, Shirley had pulled Corinne into an embrace so tight that she'd somehow gotten her arms wrapped underneath the elderly woman's Kente shawl. Shirley untangled herself then readjusted the shawl and smoothed it down the sides of Corrine's shoulders.

"God bless you a million times over."

"What was that all about?" Joy asked as they hurried off.

Once they were in the car, Shirley reached for the two containers of cupcakes on the backseat and handed one to Joy. "I say we propose a toast with cupcakes to celebrate solving another clue."

Joy popped open her container and pulled out a red velvet cupcake. "I'm not sure what you mean, but I'll never pass an opportunity to eat a cupcake."

Shirley held her cupcake in the air and tapped it against Joy's. Cream cheese frosting smeared across her fingertips, which she happily cleaned off the way she used to clean the mixer beaters when her mother baked cakes.

"I have to admit it. These are delicious," Joy said. "It's a shame that we don't have any additional vendor spaces for Poppy's Sweet Shoppe."

"I might be more apt to agree with you if she hadn't had such a sour attitude." Shirley frowned when she recalled her confrontation with the rather aggressive business owner. But Shirley refused to let that stop her from enjoying the moist, spongy cake wrapped in the red and green polka-dotted paper.

"So tell me why we're celebrating early," Joy said.

Shirley held out her arm and wiggled her wrist. "The artistry of sweetgrass basketry has been passed along for generations. It's crossed the oceans because of the African origin and the history in motion part of the clue is probably referring to the unique weaving process. I'll have to wait until tomorrow, but now I know exactly where to go."

Chapter Fifteen

THERE WAS NOTHING SHIRLEY HAD been able to do to alleviate the horrible pain. Her stomach felt like it was tied in knots. She didn't have the energy to make it to the restroom another time, and she'd made countless trips back and forth during the night. She felt horrible that she'd kept her mother awake, but as a mother always did, despite a child's age, Mama refused to leave her side.

Her mother had crawled into the bed beside her. Even though sweat beaded on Shirley's forehead, her shoulders shook with the chills. It was a terrible combination of symptoms that she wouldn't wish on her worst enemy.

"Baby, I want you to sip some water."

Shirley knew she should do it to help prevent dehydration, but what might follow wouldn't be pretty. Her mouth was dry like someone had stuffed it with a handful of cotton balls.

"I can't, Mama. I feel horrible," she whined.

Shirley knew how frustrating it was to have patients who didn't want to follow her instructions and medical knowledge. Now she was causing the frustration that irritated her mother.

By five o'clock Tuesday morning, Shirley knew she'd never make it in to work. She texted the nursing supervisor to let her know to call in a replacement. By six thirty, Shirley felt that maybe the only way she would get relief was with intravenous fluids. She couldn't sit up in bed without a dizzying headache.

When the doorbell rang at seven thirty, Shirley didn't give a second thought to who it was. Her mother shuffled to the door, and when she returned, Garrison followed behind her. He stopped at the door, his large presence filling up most of the frame. He was already dressed for work, but he hadn't put on his tie or suit jacket.

"Do I look as horrible as I feel?" Shirley asked.

"I don't think you really want me to answer that question." He chuckled.

"You're right." Shirley smiled weakly but couldn't muster a laugh.

Garrison walked to the foot of the bed. Her mother had snugly tucked her blanket under her feet the way she'd always liked it. Garrison squeezed her toes.

"I'm headed in to work," he said. "I think you should go to the emergency room. So does your mama."

Where would she muster the energy? How would she get dressed? How could she make it all the way there without a bag for the car? Shirley groaned as her stomach did another flip. She closed her eyes.

"Maybe I'll be okay. Give it some time."

Shirley felt a cool towel on the back of her neck. "You're a horrible patient," her mother said. "You'll feel much better a lot sooner if you go to the ER. You'll be in good hands. You, of all people, know that."

It was true. And more importantly, she needed to recover for the sake of twenty-five million dollars for her beloved Mercy Hospital.

Her head spun just thinking of all the programs and upgrades that could materialize at Mercy with that money. In fact, her head was *already* spinning.

"I'll go," Shirley said, her voice barely above a whisper.

She pulled on the most comfortable clothes her mother could find. The faded gray sweatpants drooped loosely around her waist, but she tied them as tight as comfort would allow. Her mother helped her into a T-shirt, then tugged a sweatshirt over her head.

She ran her hands across the top of her head then leaned back against the headboard and rested a moment before Garrison came back into the room to help her stand. She stepped into her nurse clogs, and he cradled her elbow to help guide her to the front door.

"Oh, don't forget these," her mother said. She handed Shirley's purse, phone, and a plastic bag to Garrison. "The bag is for any issues that might come up on the way."

"Thank you, Mama."

The last thing Shirley remembered was climbing into Garrison's truck. The next time she opened her eyes, Katie, one of her nurse colleagues, stood at the passenger's side door with a wheelchair.

"They're going to go ahead and take you back to triage and then get you into a room," Garrison said with a worried look on his handsome face.

"You can go. I know you have tons to do," Shirley said when she realized Garrison was following behind the wheelchair.

"Do you hear how she's trying to boss me?" Garrison asked Katie. "I'm the man in charge right now."

Shirley looked over her shoulder and playfully rolled her eyes.

"I'm not going to say a word," Katie said. "Let's get you in here and see what's going on."

"Food poisoning," Shirley assessed. "I'll probably need an IV."

"That's funny," Katie said. "I put your friend Joy on an IV about an hour ago."

Shirley shifted in the wheelchair to give her back some relief. "Joy is in the ER? Joy from the gift shop?"

"Yes," Katie said. "I think there's a bed available beside her. I can roll you by there to say hello if you're up to it, but let me get you checked in first."

Of course she wanted to see Joy. This was terrible. Absolutely terrible.

Shirley thought about the night before as Katie wrapped a blood pressure cuff around Shirley's arm. She thought about their cupcake toast. Was that what had landed both of them here in Mercy's emergency room? Lyla's cupcakes?

"Shirley, your blood pressure and heart rate just spiked."

"I'm sorry," Shirley said. "Give me a moment and take it again." Shirley took a deep breath in through her nose and exhaled slowly out of her mouths, eight times. It was a calming technique she'd learned years ago during her nursing exams. Yet she couldn't stop herself from wondering whether Lyla Poppy's annoyance at not being able to participate in the Christmas tree festival and then again not being chosen as a vendor at the holiday market would drive her to retaliate on the women some kind of way. Maybe her cupcakes weren't really a bribe or an apology after all. Maybe they were revenge. The thought that someone would go to such sinister lengths to boost business gave her chills—even more than she already had.

"It's still high, but I'll keep an eye on it," Katie said, releasing the pressure of the cuff. "Everyone gets white coat anxiety from time to time. Even nurses."

Katie rolled Shirley down the hallway. Shirley spotted Garrison near the nurses' station, but he was engulfed in a conversation with Dr. Barnhardt. Katie slowed at a curtain, announced herself, then pushed the curtain open. She stuck her head inside.

"You have a visitor, Joy."

"Oh, Joy," Shirley said at the sight of her friend. She looked exhausted, but her countenance still brightened when Katie pushed Shirley into the room.

"It looks like we may have had the same kind of night," Joy said weakly. An IV line ran from Joy's arm to a bag of saline solution hanging above her head.

"How do you feel now?"

"Better than I did when Sabrina brought me in. I hated to disturb her, but it's a scary feeling being sick when no one else is in the house. Roger had to go out of town two days ago, but his flight lands later this morning. He said he's headed over as soon as he steps foot on the ground."

"Then I know you'll be in good hands," Shirley said. "Roger will make sure you're taken care of."

"Yes, he will," Joy said, her head slightly leaning to the side.

Shirley could tell her friend was sleepy.

"Joy, we need to talk later," Shirley said. "The cupcakes. We both had one."

Joy's eyes widened. She tried to pull herself up but didn't seem to have enough energy.

"Rest," Shirley said. "Do you have your phone?"

Joy gestured toward the phone, propped between a cup of ice chips, crackers, and a can of ginger ale. "What are we going to do about the plan for today?"

"I'm leaving here later, even if I have to crawl out on my hands and knees," Shirley said. It was an overly confident statement. The way she was feeling now she didn't have the strength to stand, crawl, or roll.

Katie wheeled her into the neighboring spot and helped her out of the wheelchair and into the bed. She covered her with a sheet and two hospital-grade blankets, but that wasn't enough. Shirley's shivers had returned, and the blankets might as well have been paper. No wonder patients always asked for extra ones.

"I'll bring you a blanket from the warming unit," Katie said, without being asked. "I'm going to have an order put in for IV fluids and something for your nausea."

Shirley nodded. All she wanted to do was sleep. She wanted to say asleep until her stomach stopped turning flips, her headache disappeared, and she had enough energy to keep her eyes open for more than five minutes.

Garrison appeared in the area carrying the warm blanket Katie had promised, but before Shirley dozed off, she sent out a group text. WHATEVER YOU DO, DON'T EAT THE CUPCAKES.

"I can't definitely blame it on the cupcakes, but whatever it was did you in for a while," Dr. Barnhardt said.

He tapped on the screen of the electronic tablet in his hand. Shirley had heard he'd once been one of the loudest opponents of the hospital transferring to digital records, but now he navigated everything with ease. He scratched his gray temple, then continued to tap the screen of the tablet.

"I've put in your discharge orders. You should be cleared to leave shortly."

With that said, Dr. Barnhardt pulled a pen and notepad from his white coat pocket. He scribbled across it, ripped out the sheet, and gave it to Shirley. "Here's your prescription. It's probably the only one I ever prescribe that can't be filled by the pharmacy."

"'Rest,'" Shirley read. "You're a funny man when you choose to be, Dr. Barnhardt."

"I don't want to see your face around here for at least another day. I would say two, but knowing you, you won't follow doctor's orders. I gave Joy the same prescription," Dr. Barnhardt said. He crossed his arms and stared at Shirley. "If my memory serves me correctly, you have about five days remaining to pull off the next Mercy miracle. A Christmas miracle if I've ever seen one."

"That it is," her mother chimed in.

Mama had been sitting quietly in the corner for the last two hours. She'd convinced Dot to drop her off at the emergency room. She'd come equipped with ginger chews, saltines, a pair of fuzzy socks, and a sherpa-lined flannel blanket for Shirley. For herself she'd packed a large-print word search book, bottled water, an oatmeal cookie, and a *Women's Day* magazine.

"And you're right. She's not going to rest like she should. I'll keep an eye on her though," Mama promised. She flipped the magazine pages without looking up. "I won't let her overextend herself. I'm not going to leave her side, I can promise you that."

"Regina, I believe you wholeheartedly." Dr. Barnhardt turned to Shirley. "You know you can always text me if something else comes up, but I believe this episode has blown over. You know the routine—liquids like water, broths, and electrolytes. Eat food like crackers and toast until your stomach is more settled."

"Thank you," Shirley said.

"Now if you'll excuse me, your fan club is outside," Dr. Barnhardt said. He exited the room and Garrison, Anne, and Evelyn piled in. With her mother sitting in the corner, there was barely enough room for everyone to stand.

"We haven't wanted to disturb you this whole time, but I'm happy to see your face," Evelyn said. "I was worried about you. Both you and Joy."

"How is Joy?" Shirley asked.

Shirley was feeling much better and chomping at the bit to get busy. They were supposed to set up for the holiday market this afternoon.

"I dropped her off at home with chicken noodle soup from the cafeteria. I took her extra key and told her I'd stop by after I left work," Anne said. "We sat and chatted for a while when we first got there. She told me about your visit with Corrine."

"Right now I'm more concerned about the cupcakes. Please tell me you didn't eat them."

"Thank goodness neither of us did," Anne said, looking at Evelyn. "Ralph and I attended a holiday party at church, and I didn't have room for another bite."

"I went back to my office after our meeting yesterday and accidentally left them behind on my desk," Evelyn said. "As soon as I saw your text this morning, I dumped them in the trash. I didn't think twice about it."

Garrison held up his hand. "Something sounds fishy. What cupcakes? What's going on?"

Mama closed her magazine and sat forward in the chair. "I have the same questions."

Shirley not only told them about her suspicions about the cupcake but outlined everything that had transpired the evening before, even up to the point when she realized Corrine didn't hold the next clue but had unknowingly pointed her in a different direction. The bracelet, Shirley said, had directed her to the Charleston City Market, and that was where she was headed as soon as her discharge papers were in hand.

Her mother hadn't uttered a word other than to make sure Shirley felt all right. Like she'd promised Dr. Barnhardt, she'd been by her daughter's side the entire time. Dot too.

They followed behind her like a shadow at high noon, walking in and out of the artists' booths, admiring their handiwork but not assisting Shirley in anyway. Dot talked about how she needed to cook three sweet potato pies before Christmas Eve, and her mother's focus was finding a bag of stone-ground grits.

Then suddenly Shirley spotted them. They were known at the Charleston City Market as the basket ladies, but Shirley's vivid memories dated back to the time in her childhood when she'd see quaint roadside stands along the highway. Back then, the intricately woven baskets hung from wooden boards under homemade painted signs. She'd never known a time when they didn't have them in their home—hanging on the wall as decor, holding scraps of her mother's quilting fabrics and threads or temporarily housing fresh squash, zucchini, or potatoes from the bounty of their family's and friends' gardens.

Shirley knew the origin of the baskets and how the Gullah community in the Low Country preserved the skills that descendants had passed down from West Africa. But who among them held the clue?

One beautiful brown-skinned woman offered up a gap-toothed smile as Shirley walked past. Her fingers, almost seemingly bent from working years at the craft, coiled the sweetgrass into a signature circular design. It was second nature for her, woven into her soul as tightly as the palmetto fronds in the basket at her feet that she would use later to fortify the basket.

"Are you looking for something special, sweetheart?" the woman asked.

"I am. But not in the way you might think," Shirley said.

"Really, now?" the woman said.

"I'm hoping to find someone whose family has been weaving baskets for five generations."

The woman's laughter brightened her eyes. "Take your pick," she said. "What is it that you want to know, because you look like you're from around here. I'd be surprised if you didn't know someone already."

"Charleston born and bred," Shirley said. "How did you guess?"

"I can tell. A sense about you." Her bronze-colored bangles clanked as she worked. "I'm Ida."

"Nice to meet you, Ida. I'm Shirley. And for the record, your work is stunning. I'm always amazed by the beauty and designs of these baskets." Shirley watched in silence as Ida and the other ladies at the open booths around her crafted their items. They were able to weave, tend to browsing customers, and tell the stories of the baskets to tourists who were Christmas shopping.

Shirley's gaze traveled to a girl weaving at a corner table. She couldn't have been older than seventeen or eighteen. Shirley walked closer to her table and noticed that she was intertwining her sweet-grass with a gold fiber. In fact, all the creations at her table had the gold fiber woven throughout.

"Hello." Her voice sounded as soft as her honey-colored skin looked. Her high cheekbones and round brown eyes were untouched by age and worry. She wore her hair in big coils that were held off her face with an elastic headband.

"I love the gold in your work."

"It pays homage to the Gold Coast of West Africa, where my family originates from."

"You look too young to have perfected this art," Shirley said, admiring her work.

"You definitely won't find most eighteen-year-olds doing this on a Tuesday night," she said. She put down the project she was working on and wiggled her fingers. She twisted the top off a jar and rubbed a cream salve between her fingers and massaged it into her palm. "I love creating things with my hands. I sew, paint, and make pottery and jewelry."

"That's amazing," Shirley said. She gave kudos to any teenager with interests other than technology and the latest social media challenge. "If your work is anything like your baskets, I'm sure it's all gorgeous. I'd love to see and support your artistry."

"I'm about to put my art out there for the first time. I mean, other than these baskets. But these come easy to me, and everyone always loves them. They practically sell themselves. My business is called Noelle's Artistry and Designs." She slid a square card out of her back pocket and gave it to Shirley. "If you scan the QR code on the card it will take you to my website, which went live today. My friend did it for me. She's just starting out. It's not anything super fancy. Yet."

"I remember this business. I'm on the committee for the holiday market. Didn't you miss the meeting?"

"I did," Noelle said. She looked like she was slightly embarrassed. "I slept right through it. I was still recovering from my exams."

"I remember the days," Shirley said. "And I love your name, by the way."

The name brought back memories of the day Shirley learned that "The First Noel" was one of Mr. Christmas's favorite songs.

The July sunlight spilled through the floor-to-ceiling windows of the hospital room. Despite the natural light and relentless heat of the summer, Mr. Benjamin Christmas's room had been transformed into a scene that rivaled a Christmas card. A Christmas tree stood in each corner, the largest of which had a Polar Express *train that circled the base.*

"Mr. Christmas has really outdone himself," Shirley said. "I know he told me he wanted to have Christmas in July, but I didn't expect all of this."

"He said he's always lived his life in a big way. I guess this is no exception," Garrison said. He handed Shirley a plate with shrimp and pineapple skewers, salmon croquets, and yellow rice. It was scanty in comparison to his own plate that had a mountain of food.

Mr. Christmas had been positioned in the middle of all the action, where he could turn his wheelchair around at will. His family members were easy to spot. They were all dressed in matching red polo-style short-sleeved shirts and khaki bottoms, and all seemed to be having a fairly good time. Except for Nicholas Christmas.

He walked up to Garrison.

"I apologize for all of this. My father tends to go overboard when it comes to Christmas." He mumbled under his breath, "As with everything else."

"It looks like he's enjoying himself," Shirley said. "He's had a rough couple of days."

"My father will bounce back. He always does. Even at his age. Do you think he'd want to leave his estate in my hands? Not a chance. He'd give it all away before he let me inherit my just portion."

Shirley bit her lip. The last thing she would do was voice her opinion on another family's business.

They stood in awkward silence for what was probably a few seconds, but felt more like a few minutes.

"You should've seen the faces of the children in the pediatric units today when Santa and his elves arrived pulling wagons full of gifts," Garrison said. "Everyone was crying—the children, their parents, the nurses, and the physicians. I even shed a tear. Or two. Or five."

Nicholas huffed. "I'm not surprised. Dad is always looking to make a big impression."

Or is it that he has a big heart? *Shirley thought. She didn't want to entertain any negative conversations, even as a bystander. She'd only known Mr. Christmas for seven months, but even in his failing health he'd been sweet and kind. Many patients were the opposite— ornery and impatient when they were faced with uncertainty.*

"Great," Nicholas muttered.

What now? *Shirley thought. This man was determined to be grumpy in a room full of Christmas cheer, twinkling lights, and even baby Jesus. Across the room in the Nativity scene, the swaddled new-born was wrapped tightly and lying in a manger with Mary, Joseph, and the three wise men looking down at Him in adoration.*

"I was told Tatum wouldn't be in attendance. But as usual, he's found a way to stay connected to us. A bumbling fool is what he is. Unfortunately my granddaughter, Madeline, has fallen in love with him. And to make matters worse, he's the third Tatum. You'd think his family could think of a different name."

So that was the Tatum that Mr. Christmas had spoken of. Tatum was part of the Christmas family's legal team and helped to oversee their estate planning, a job that had been passed down to him and his father when the eldest Tatum retired.

Shirley was looking for a way to excuse herself when she noticed Mr. Christmas beckoning from across the room. His smile and eyes were bright. That was another reason why Shirley knew this day gave him the lift he needed.

"Christmas isn't Christmas unless someone sings 'The First Noel,'" Mr. Christmas said. *"It's my absolute favorite song for the holidays. Even if it's Christmas in July. Shirley, would you do me the honors?"*

How could Shirley deny his request? She wouldn't. So after Mr. Christmas gathered everyone around, she closed her eyes and pulled the song from her soul, as if it were the last song she would ever sing, and the last song Mr. Christmas would ever hear.

"That's me—Noelle. Daughter of Nancy. Granddaughter of Nadine. Great-granddaughter of Naomi and great-great-granddaughter of Nora. Five generations. And in case you're wondering, if I have a daughter her name will not start with N. It stops here with me."

"Five generations," Shirley said, standing up straighter. "Noelle, do you have anything else in gold that I might want?"

Noelle shrugged and shook her head thoughtfully. "We only weave the gold threads through our baskets, and these are all we sell here. Maybe you can try the jewelry boutique at the end of the aisle. That's where I got this." She raised her hand and showed Shirley a gold thumb ring. "It looks like it's only a design, but if you look close you can tell it's a line of connected scripted *N*s. We all have them."

"Beautiful," Shirley said.

"Hey there," a woman walked up and stood behind Noelle. She had the same crown of thick curls but with a streak of gray at the front temple.

"Hi, Mom," Noelle said.

"I was admiring your daughter's ring," Shirley said. "And your baskets, of course."

"Can I wrap one up for you?" Nancy asked. "Or we have nice gold boxes, depending on the size of the basket."

"I would definitely like a gold box, if you have one. One that's specifically for me—Shirley Bashore."

"Shirley Bashore," the woman said her name like she was an old classmate she'd reunited with at her twenty-fifth class reunion. "Why didn't you say something, Noelle?"

"Mom, I don't ask the name of everyone who walks up. And besides, why would I?"

"You don't remember what I told you about Shirley Bashore?"

Noelle shrugged again. "Sorry. The only thing that has been on my mind for the past month is physics, calculus, and writing informative texts."

Nancy knelt and reached under the table and produced a large sweetgrass basket with a lid. She plopped the basket down on the table, lifted the lid, and reached inside. Shirley could have screamed in delight. She knew it. She knew she'd been right.

Her mother and Dot appeared from nowhere. Her mother gave her two thumbs-up, and Dot feigned like she was wiping sweat from her forehead.

"Ms. Bashore, maybe I'll see you at the holiday market."

"You most certainly will," Shirley said.

"It must be a popular event," Noelle said before Shirley started to walk away. "A woman called me yesterday and asked me if I'd be willing to give up my spot. She knew I'd missed the meeting. It was really weird."

There was no question who the mysterious woman was.

So, not only was she trying to poison people, but she was harassing the vendors who were chosen to be in the holiday market. When they'd kicked her out of the meeting, she'd run out with the full version of the contact list, and she was using it to her full advantage. Shirley's stomach twisted, but this time it was from anger.

"Don't worry about Lyla Poppy," Shirley told Noelle. "I'll see you tomorrow. If you bring that pretty smile with you, I'm sure you'll sell out of everything you have."

"Nice meeting you, and Godspeed in all that you do, Shirley Bashore," Nancy said. "You were chosen for a reason, and God will see to it that you finish the task."

"I need that same kind of confidence," Shirley said.

"No," Nancy said. "You need that same kind of faith."

"You're right," Shirley said. "Thanks for the reminder."

Shirley pushed her way through the growing crowd until she reached her mother and Dot. They'd found a bench to rest their legs and also participate in one of their favorite pastimes—people watching.

"My goodness, Shirley," Mama said. "When you said you were going to see Corrine, I nearly had to bite my lip to keep from spilling the beans. Thank God you figured it out."

"I never doubted you," Dot said. "I've been sending up some mighty prayers for you and Mercy Hospital."

"I appreciate every prayer," Shirley said, sandwiching herself between the two ladies. She couldn't wait to get home and lie down. She'd probably overdone it. Dr. Barnhardt had been right about her. She hadn't done well at following the doctor's orders.

"Baby doll, would you mind dropping us off at the Dock Street Theater? We have our final play rehearsal this evening, and we're going to run the entire performance in full costume."

"No problem." Shirley stood and helped her elderly bodyguards to their feet. They were supposed to head to the exit, but that was hard to do when her mother wanted to stop and browse at every booth. Shirley was two steps from whining about it all when she spotted it. Garrison's Christmas gift. She always said she would know it when she saw it. It was meaningful. It was perfect.

Her mother walked up to the counter as she was completing her purchase.

"Who is that for?" she asked.

"It's Garrison's Christmas gift."

Her mother didn't seem impressed, but there was more behind the story than she realized. Shirley dismissed her unenthusiastic response.

"All of that thinking, and this is what you thunk?" She chuckled.

"Really, mother? He's going to love it. I'm sure of it."

Her mother shrugged. "Whatever suits your fancy. Let me find Dot. We don't want to be late for rehearsal."

"I'm right behind you," Dot said, walking up. She jiggled her car keys and handed them to Shirley. "Don't worry about coming back to pick us up. You should get your rest. I'll have Sylvester drop us back to your house."

Dot pulled her purse up on her shoulder. "And don't look at your mother like that. Sylvester is my *friend*."

Shirley wasn't sure about that. Shirley had noticed how Sylvester was conveniently waiting for Dot following every church service.

He'd been a widower for over ten years, and according to Mama, he'd never shown interest in anyone else. Until now.

"I haven't said a word, Dot."

Dot let Mama take the front seat, and she slipped into the back to stretch out her legs. "That's funny. Does anyone else smell a pipe?"

Her words made Shirley pause. She inhaled. It was faint. But it was definitely there. She locked the door and pulled away from the curb, watching in the rearview and side mirrors to make sure they didn't have anyone following them.

Her mother warmed up her vocal cords on the ride to the Dock Street Theater. She only had three speaking lines, but she was tapped to sing one of the solos. She popped a lemon ginger lozenge into her mouth and hummed until Shirley pulled in front of the loading zone on Church Street.

"Well, can we hear the other clue, or what?" Dot asked. "We've proven that we can hold our tongues, haven't we?"

"You took the words right out of my mouth," her mother said. She unbuckled her seat belt and shifted in her seat toward Shirley. "You said yourself that you only feel comfortable reading the clues to people who you know won't try anything fishy or try to help you."

"Since you two have proven that you can follow the rules, I'll read it," Shirley said.

"'Though once it fell to ruin, its majesty is now restored. The city keeps it in the light to prove the world is yours.'"

Chapter Sixteen

"You absolutely won't believe what has happened," Evelyn said.

Shirley and Evelyn stood in the atrium waiting for their two friends to arrive. Under the doctor's orders and their friends' insistence, Shirley and Joy had taken the morning and most of the early afternoon to recuperate. Shirley had enjoyed a breakfast of oatmeal, toast, and tea with honey. She felt 100 percent better than she had the previous morning. She looked better too. Her countenance reflected it. She'd called to check on Joy and was happy to hear that Roger had arrived at her house earlier that morning with breakfast in hand and intentions to keep her company for as long as she needed it. When Joy decided to meet them at the hospital, Roger said he would stay behind to fix the leak he'd discovered under her kitchen sink.

Garrison had a dozen red roses delivered to her midday, lifting her spirits even more. On her way in to the hospital, she'd picked up Joy, who had gone directly to check on the gift shop. Shirley had gone straight to the Mercy Christmas tree and hung the miniature sweetgrass basket ornament she'd received from Nancy and Noelle.

"It's absolutely beautiful in here. I don't see anything wrong," Shirley said.

"You don't see anything," Evelyn said. She pressed a finger to her lips. "But do you hear anything?"

Shirley closed her eyes, listening carefully. A giggling child. The hum of the automatic floor sweeper being pushed by Earl, one of the custodians. Muted conversations of the guests passing through en route to various places in the hospital. Birds.

Birds?

"I hear birds," Shirley said.

"You have a good ear, Shirley," Evelyn said. "We don't just have a partridge in a pear tree. We have an entire family of birds that have nested in the tippy top of the Audubon Society's tree."

"How did they manage to build a nest that quickly?"

"Your guess is as good as mine. All I know is that we need to find a way to safely remove them, and the sooner the better."

"Let's tell Earl and have him call a bird removal company. I remember Daddy had to call one once when he and Mama had a bird stuck in the chimney years ago. Mama called me in Atlanta hysterical and refused to leave her bedroom until the bird was gone."

"I like that idea. I was thinking of contacting animal control, but your option may be better."

"I'm on it," Shirley said. "If Earl reaches them right away they may be able to get here today."

"That would be ideal. The maintenance and custodial staff have already set up tables for the holiday market, and the vendors are starting to arrive. The last thing I want to think about are birds on the loose."

Five minutes later, Shirley had talked to the head custodian, he'd called a bird removal company, and they'd promised to come out as soon as possible.

"We're all set," Shirley said after Earl texted her. "They'll be here in the next hour, and the even better part about it is that it's on the house. The owner had surgery here last month and raved about the exemplary care he received."

"Speaking of exemplary care," Evelyn said, "James is treating Queen Victoria like royalty. They've taken over the house. He spends so much time with her that I'm starting to get a little jealous."

"Mama's pup is going to be hard pressed to leave," Shirley said.

"I'm starting to think James might pack a bag and move right along with her," Evelyn joked.

The trees in the Mercy Christmas tree festival had become quite the highlight for visitors. Guests milled through the displays, expressing admiration and reading about the organizations and businesses that the trees represented. Word had gotten around the city, and people were visiting the hospital just to see the Christmas trees.

And they weren't coming empty-handed. They came with ornaments, filling the branches of the Mercy Christmas tree until some of them drooped. It wasn't as easy for Shirley to spot the branches where she'd hung the ornaments she'd found from her mission. They were hidden somewhere behind ornaments like the handmade reindeer, the cello hung by the Charleston Symphony Orchestra, and the gamecock wearing a University of South Carolina Christmas sweater.

Shirley noticed Buddy from across the atrium, and he was headed their way. He used his hand to smooth over the few wisps of brunette hairs that remained on the top of his head.

"Hi, Shirley. Hi, Evelyn," Buddy said. He rubbed his hands together as if he were up to something. "I hate to bother you, but I wanted to see if there's a way that you can put me on the program for Saturday's Hot Cocoa Toast. I have a solo that I'd like to sing. An original song that I've been working on all month. And no worries about music accompaniment. I can sing a cappella."

Evelyn cleared her throat and looked away. Shirley knew what that meant. It would be her responsibility to break the news.

"Buddy, we've pretty much finalized the program. We don't have room to add anything else. What happened to singing with the Mercy Hospital Chorale?"

Buddy turned his head and looked around as if he wanted to make sure he wasn't being watched. "I don't want to sound petty, but not everyone appreciates my God-given talents. They said that only ten people were allowed to sing with the chorale at the Hot Cocoa Toast. Is that true?"

"Uh…" Shirley paused. She hadn't told them any such thing. Kaye, the director, made the rules, and from the sound of it, she'd ruled Buddy out.

Evelyn jumped in to save her. "We're on strict time constraints for Saturday evening. I'm afraid a solo won't be possible. I can ask Kaye to reconsider, but I can't make any promises."

Buddy shrugged. "You don't know what you're missing by not letting me sing, but I suppose I have no other choice. I was already planning to debut my new song at the Christmas program at church on Sunday, but I haven't heard from our chorus director there, either. I've called him four times already."

"Patience is key," Shirley said. "It'll all work out like it should. Talk to you later, Buddy. It was good seeing you."

"Sometimes some of the best advice we can take is our own," Evelyn said. "Everything is going to work out. There are only two clues left. Can you believe it?"

"Two more clues and four more days."

Shirley spotted Joy and Anne rounding the corner. Joy was holding a copy of the *Charleston Buzz*, and she handed the folded paper to Shirley. "I know how you love reading your paper. And I even have it opened to your favorite section—the restaurant health inspection reports."

"You know me well." Shirley smiled. She glanced at the page, and an article caught her attention. She frowned, then stopped to peruse it.

"What is it, Shirley?" Joy asked.

"There was a food poisoning outbreak last week, and many of the affected people came to Mercy Hospital to get treated. They were able to trace the outbreak back to that little lunch spot about two blocks down. One of the nurses ran out for food, and I gave her money to bring me back one of the lunch combos. I didn't get to finish all of it, but I ate the majority. That was the same day I got sick."

Joy walked nearer and looked over Shirley's shoulder. "My goodness. I ate there too. I ran out and picked up lunch because I didn't feel like eating my leftovers."

"So we ate at the same place on the same day," Shirley concluded. "And we were both sick on the same night. I'd say that restaurant was the culprit, and not Lyla. Mama tried to tell me that it was a long shot that I'd gotten sick from eating cupcakes."

"And it also means I threw away three perfectly delicious cupcakes for nothing."

"They were very delicious," Shirley said with a soft chuckle. "Delicious but not poisonous."

"This is good news," Anne said, leading the ladies out to the Grove. "We might as well take advantage of this beautiful weather before the cold front blows in this weekend. I heard this morning that we might have a few flurries headed our way."

"My mother and I are probably the only people in the city who actually want the snow," Shirley said.

"I'd welcome the snow. It's the ice and sleet that I don't want to deal with. This Texan woman feels better in humidity and sunshine," Joy said.

The bush-lined pathways were usually trimmed with seasonal flowers in full bloom, but now the bushes were flounced with strings of lights, which were lit at night. The famed and historic Mercy Angel stood sentinel as always. It had recently been pressure washed, blasting away the summer and fall pollens.

"Our tree arrived just in time," Shirley said, admiring the Murray cypress laid on the bed of a nearby truck. It was secured to the flatbed trailer with ropes, and the root ball was wrapped tightly with burlap.

At Aurora's thoughtful suggestion, the tree had already been wrapped with white twinkling lights. They only needed to plant it in the hole dug by the Mercy statue, then hang the ornaments. Shirley assumed that was what the ladder leaning against the truck was for.

The ladies found a table where they could keep an eye on the action.

"Mr. Christmas loved coming to sit out here. It was one of the last areas he came to enjoy before his health began to really fail him and he couldn't be transported as easily. I remember I was sitting out here with him when Mama called and told me she'd gotten the news about her landing a solo in the Christmas play. He was thrilled, even though Christmas was still months away. I'd told him so much about Mama and how I'd prayed that the city would get the opportunity to hear her voice. He told me he wished he could be there but didn't think he would be."

"He would probably love that they're planting this tree in the Grove," Anne said.

Shirley nodded. "Absolutely. He told me this area would be a place of new beginnings. I'm not sure what Mr. Christmas meant by that, but I'm keeping my eyes open for the signs."

The crew worked skillfully, and soon the tree was planted in the hole they'd prepared. The ladies had been lost in their own thoughts for a while before Shirley quietly read the clue again.

"'Though once it fell to ruin, its majesty is now restored. The city keeps it in the light to prove the world is yours.'"

"The first thing that comes to mind for me is a lighthouse," Evelyn said. "Once upon a time, our lighthouses—like most—were in dire conditions. Usually the government is involved with restoring and repairing them."

"The Sullivan's Island Lighthouse is called the Charleston Light," Anne added. "Addie did a report on it in September, and we drove out to get some pictures of her out there. They turned out beautiful, but other than that, there's not much to do."

Shirley drummed her fingers on the table. "'The city keeps it in the light to prove the world is yours.' The lighthouse makes as much sense as anything else."

"I agree. But there are so many things that have been brought to ruins in Charleston by our historic fires, by hurricanes," Joy said. "This is a good option."

"I pray it's the only option," Shirley said.

A low bed pickup truck arrived carrying bins of oversized red ornaments. Two men hopped out and set up an adjustable scaffold that wrapped around the tree.

Joy snapped her fingers. "That reminds me. Did you put the last ornament on the tree?"

"As soon as I got here."

"I know one thing. I moved to Charleston over a year ago, and I still haven't purchased a sweetgrass basket," Joy said.

"It's basically a rite of passage to have a sweetgrass basket in Charleston. It's not just a tradition, it's a requirement," Anne said. "We'll have to fix that."

"But at least you have a sweetgrass *bracelet*," Shirley reminded her about their trip to Corinne's. "I, for one, wouldn't mind having earrings to match."

Evelyn held up her hand. "Even though I now feel the need to find a sweetgrass brooch to add to my collection, we have to focus, ladies. Two of us need to stay here to make sure all our vendors have everything they need. I wouldn't mind going out to the lighthouse, but I think it's best if I stay here."

"Then it's my turn to go along with Shirley," Anne volunteered. "Let me make sure I've taken care of all of my delivery orders and discharges." She put a hand on Shirley's arm. "Would you mind dropping me home after?"

"I don't mind at all. And we should get a move on things. I need to be home early to make sure Mama has everything she needs for the play tonight."

"From what I can recall, this is the first time they've had a Christmas performance like this one," Evelyn said. "And it's the last show of the season. The theater will be closed until the new year."

A collaboration of churches around Charleston had joined together for a theatrical musical production of the Nativity. It had been marketed as an experience of faith infused with cultural splendor. Her mother wouldn't reveal anything about the performance, but according to an article Shirley had read in the *Charleston Buzz*, it was tapped to be a spectacular show for anyone lucky enough to have a ticket.

"Keep us posted on anything exciting that happens," Evelyn said as she and Joy stood to head back into the hospital.

"You too," Shirley said. "Let us know if the birds are still on the loose."

"What?" Joy exclaimed. "No one told me about any birds."

"I'll tell you one thing. It's not a partridge in a pear tree or two turtledoves." Evelyn looped her arm through Joy's. "It'll be taken care of soon. Shirley has already made the call to the removal company. Now let her take care of the next clue too."

"Birds. Birds in the hospital. Birds out here. The *only* things out here besides us are birds," Shirley said, staring upward. Seagulls glided through the sky like kites without strings. They swooped in unison and squawked in delight.

It was a beautiful sight, yet Shirley held back her tears. She was a mix of emotions. Happy because she'd come this far, frustrated that she still felt far from the finish line, even though only this current clue and one more remained.

Shirley trudged around the surrounding grounds in the area, and Anne followed not far behind. She stopped at the fence surrounding the lighthouse. It was painted black at the top and white at the bottom, though she remembered once when her father told her it had originally been hideous orange that everyone complained about, him included.

"Lord," she whispered, "please help me. Show me the light. Give me a sign."

Anne walked up quietly behind Shirley. "It looks like we have company."

Chapter Seventeen

"Nicholas?"

Shirley hadn't seen the younger Christmas since the night of the party, when the details of her adventure were revealed. Since Benjamin couldn't be here, his son would do.

"What a wonderful surprise," Shirley said, shaking Nicholas's hand. "Is something wrong?"

"You could say that," Nicholas said. He adjusted his brown fedora.

Shirley looked around to see if someone else had come along with him. She noticed a black SUV parked nearby. It was probably his driver.

"You must have some reason for being out here. I wouldn't be here myself at this time of year unless there was a good reason. And twenty-five million dollars is a good reason."

"I realize that. And once you hear what I have to say, you'll realize that I come for a good reason as well."

"What's that?" Anne asked, stepping beside Shirley as if she would have to defend her.

Nicholas Christmas pulled a pipe from the inside pocket of his jacket.

Shirley shook her finger at Nicholas. "Have you been following me? The scent of the pipe smoke. I've been smelling it from time to time."

"I'm sorry. That's a guilty pleasure that's been following me around for years. I haven't quite been able to shake it. My father didn't approve of my habit, so in his honor, I'm attempting to cut down a bit."

"But have you been following Shirley? And why?" Anne pushed.

"Yes and no," Nicholas admitted. "I followed you to make sure you were safe from Tatum Everett III. It seems he wanted to keep an eye on you and possibly intimidate you along the way. Since he's engaged to my granddaughter, Madeline, and he's been around the family in a business capacity for quite some time, he knows a lot about our family home. However, what he's never been told is that security keeps an eye on any suspicious activity. They noticed that he would always disappear into the library to take calls whenever he was visiting. They listened to part of his conversations through our intercom system and found out he'd tried to plan some obstacles to hinder you, but they fell through. He'd even hired someone to stake outside your house with intention to start trouble, but that never played out like he hoped. They took his money and ran."

"That's horrible," Anne said.

"There was an incident in which he had someone steal a poinsettia that was intended to make it home with you. We knew it contained the clue, so I had my driver bring me to your house so I could deliver it personally. But out of sight, of course."

The black SUV, Shirley thought.

"We also caught word that he wanted to tamper with your vehicle, so we kept an eye on that as well. You were only a few steps away from me once when I was walking around your car in the

Mercy employee parking lot. Luckily, you and Mr. Baker were distracted with each other."

"I've met the younger Tatum before. Only once, but his is not a face I would forget," Shirley said, recalling the day he'd come to Garrison's office. "I've never seen him around."

Nicholas lit his pipe and took several puffs before he continued. "He knows enough to keep himself out of sight. Instead, he asked others to try to thwart your attempt. He didn't go too far, thank goodness, but the fact that he'd be willing to try anything threw up a red flag."

"So by following me, you were keeping an eye on any possible shenanigans that Tatum III may have set forth," Shirley concluded.

"Exactly," Nicholas said. "My driver and I have been very busy."

Shirley shrugged. "But why? Why would Tatum want to do anything that would prevent Mercy Hospital from receiving the money?"

Nicholas looked above his head at the squawking seagulls circling. "Because he thinks there is more money in his future. Madeline's legacy is very secure. Whomever she marries would, of course, share in that wealth to a certain degree."

"What does that have to do with the Mercy donation?"

"We didn't read this on the night of the party, but in the event that you were unable to complete the mission, the will states that the money should be moved into an established trust that can be distributed and used at Madeline's discretion."

"My goodness," Anne said. "The things people will do."

"Thankfully, Madeline ended the engagement after the younger Tatum's actions were uncovered. I think this was the thing that finally pulled the wool off her eyes, and I couldn't be more relieved. I believe she was pressuring herself because all her friends are getting married and starting families. I've told her a million times that everyone's road to happiness isn't on the same timetable."

"Never heard a statement more true," Shirley said. She sighed. "Thank you. For all you did that I didn't even know about."

Nicholas puffed on his pipe. "I should be saying the same to you, Shirley." He started walking back to the parking area, and Shirley and Anne followed in the same direction. It was time to leave. There was nothing out here for them to find.

"I don't know if you know this, but my father kept an extensive collection of journals that he's written in for years."

"I was aware," Shirley said. "I'd find him reading through them from time to time."

"Well, I'd never bothered to look in them before. After all these years," Nicholas confessed. "But since his passing, they're the things that allow me to feel closest to him." His loafers crunched across the gravel as he neared his SUV.

"I understand my father more in his death than I ever did when he was alive. I realize why he did the things he did, and why one of his greatest joys was seeing other people happy. He lived his life for others more than he did for himself."

"I found that to be true from the moment I met him," Shirley said.

"His wealth never changed him, other than to make him a man who was compassionate to meeting the needs of others and the causes he believed in. I'm sixty-eight years old, and I'm still not half the man he was."

A tear slipped from the corner of his eye. "I wish I had the chance to tell him now. I guess I didn't know how to love who he was without always being judgmental."

Anne stepped up to comfort him. "You know what, Nicholas? You can't change the past, but you still have a future to look to. One of my favorite scripture verses talks about God knowing the plans that He has for us. He wants a good future with hope in every part of our lives."

"Ah. One of my father's favorite scriptures. Jeremiah 29:11."

The driver got out and opened the back door for Nicholas, holding his pipe while his boss got settled in the back seat. "My father had great confidence in you, Shirley. The only thing you need now is that same confidence in yourself."

The driver closed the door, but Shirley watched the window glide down. "Open your eyes to everything around you," Nicholas said.

Shirley was still thinking about Nicholas's words as she slid into her front row seats at the Dock Street Theater. Once it was time for the play to begin, the houselights went down, plunging them in complete darkness. Shirley's eyes hadn't had time to adjust before a single spotlight clicked on, focusing on a wee-sized girl in the middle of the stage.

She took a deep breath before she began, as if she'd been taught to do it to calm her nerves. Compared to her size, her voice was large and impressive. She began to recite the story of the birth of Jesus that Shirley knew was from the book of Luke. The child's innocence and her apparent love from already knowing her Savior brought Shirley to tears. She could also hear sniffles coming from Joy and Anne, who were seated on either side.

As the spotlight began to fade out, a thunderous voice echoed through the theater. "For to us a child is born, to us a Son is given, and the government will be on His shoulders. And He will be called Wonderful Counselor, Mighty God."

Shirley couldn't put words to the range of emotions that she felt during the play. The coming together of different cultures, denominations, and races warmed her soul. It was a glorious production with brilliantly colored costumes, sets, and pulsating music. They intertwined classic Christmas carols with gospel-style spirituals, which was when her mother emerged from the middle of a town of Bethlehemites.

The cast clapped and swayed back and forth as her mother sang a powerful rendition of "Go Tell It on the Mountain." Their eyes connected, and Shirley knew that both of their faces lit with pride and admiration.

Shirley clasped her hands under her chin, present in the moment. By the end of the last verse the entire cast had joined the song, urging the audience to participate as well. Some of the cast began to exit the stage on either side, walking out into the audience carrying sweetgrass baskets full of gifts that they handed out randomly. When the houselights rose fully to signal intermission, Shirley spotted Garrison sitting on the end seat in the next to the last row. She was distracted by trying to get his attention, and Anne had to nudge her to get her to turn around.

"Oh!" Shirley whirled and found herself standing in front of the men who were portraying the three wise men. One of the men, who'd come bearing frankincense to Jesus, reached under his purple tunic and pulled out a gold box and envelope. He didn't speak a single word but handed her the items and disappeared backstage.

"Let's go to the lobby," she told Anne, Joy, and Evelyn. It seemed everyone else in the theater had the same idea. Try as they might, it took them some time to press through the crowd. She kept her eye on Garrison, which was easy to do because of his height, but she was surprised when it looked like he was moving toward the exit.

The doors opened, and Garrison disappeared into the night.

Where was he headed?

The crowd in the lobby was squeezed together like a tight can of sardines. Her friends headed to an empty corner.

"I'll be right back," Shirley said. She didn't expect to see Garrison by the time she made it through the packed lobby and walked out into the chilly night. She was right. He was already gone.

Shirley turned and pushed her way back through the crowd. She found Anne, Joy, and Evelyn huddled together in the far end of the room.

"Is everything all right?" Evelyn asked her.

"Everything is great. I wish there was a way I could thank Mr. Christmas, God rest his soul. He brought the answer to this clue directly to us. He knew I'd be here. I would never have missed my mother's city-wide debut." She picked up a spare program she spotted on a nearby table. "As far as I'm concerned, this is his Christmas gift to me. Either that or he figured I might be losing steam as we got toward the end."

"Whatever the case, there's only one clue to go," Anne said.

"But can anyone break down this clue we have right now? I'd be interested in knowing," Joy said.

"I've been thinking about it," Anne said. "The original Dock Street Theater was destroyed by the Great Fire of 1740. That's what the clue meant about falling to ruin. I believe the part about the majesty being restored is because it has been rebuilt and renovated by the city a few times, but it also may be a hint to its location."

"Queen Street." Evelyn nodded.

Shirley had thoughts about the last part of the clue. *The city keeps it in the light to prove the world is yours.* "There's usually a spotlight on stage. And to prove the world is yours is probably related to the Shakespearean adage that 'All the world's a stage.'"

"'All the world's a stage, and all the men and women merely players,'" Joy said. "I had to memorize part of that in one of my college classes. I can't remember how the rest goes."

"Thankfully, we don't need to know any more. We only need to focus on the last clue." Shirley ripped open the envelope but stopped before pulling out the piece of paper.

"This is the last one, ladies. I don't know what I'm feeling. I'm a ball of nerves and excitement all rolled into one."

"You described it perfectly," Evelyn said. "I'm feeling the same way."

"Me too."

"Me three."

Shirley tugged out the paper and held it where they could all see it. "'To the place where it all began, the years ahead are blessed. Underneath her gaze and an open sky, if only you'll say yes.'"

They all looked at each other in confusion. Shirley had a feeling they'd have to dig into Charleston's history for this one. What could lead them to the place of Charleston's beginning and take them years ahead to Charleston's future?

"You know what?" Anne said. "I say we enjoy the rest of the play tonight and think about this in the morning."

"Let's at least take a look at the ornament," Evelyn said.

Shirley removed the top of the gift box. "The Nativity. It's the perfect memento for tonight."

"I will never for the life of me know how Mr. Christmas was able to pull all of this together. It baffles me," Joy said.

"I'm sure there are more moving parts and more hands in this than we'll ever know," Shirley said. "But I'll always look at it as a Christmas miracle."

"Me too," Evelyn said.

The lights in the lobby blinked, signaling that the second half of the play was about to begin.

"I'm coming right behind you," Shirley said as her friends made their way back into the theater. She pulled out her phone and sent a text message to Garrison.

WHERE DID YOU DISAPPEAR TO?

He responded immediately. NEEDED TO TAKE CARE OF SOME THINGS. HATED TO RUN. GIVE YOUR MAMA MY LOVE. WILL CALL YOU LATER.

Shirley texted back a thumbs-up emoji as the lights blinked for a final time. She rushed inside, hurrying to get to her seat before the second half of the play began. She tried to stay present in the moment, but she found it hard to concentrate on anything else but the next clue.

Chapter Eighteen

Two days had passed and still none of them knew where to start. No ideas. No assumptions. No clue. If Shirley's mind were a well, then it had run dry. There was one clue remaining, and Christmas Eve was upon them.

Shirley had intended for her and Mama to ride with Garrison to Mercy's Christmas Eve tree lighting and Hot Cocoa Toast, but he'd called at the last minute to tell her he needed to head to the hospital early due to an emergency. She wanted to know specifics, especially since it was a Saturday evening, but that was neither here nor there. He certainly didn't need her approval to handle his job. He hadn't even mentioned anything else about what made him leave the play early, and neither had she.

Shirley couldn't help but feel he'd been standoffish most of the day—busy when she called him this morning, turning down lunch with her in exchange for making a sandwich at home, and now this. He hadn't even seemed bothered when she expressed her concern about the last clue.

"I wouldn't worry about it," Garrison had said. "Mr. Christmas never intended for you to fail. You were one of his favorite people. He wouldn't let that happen."

"Are you sure about that?" Shirley had asked. "You do realize I have one day remaining, right? *One day.*"

Garrison hadn't responded. Shirley wished she could see his face. She wanted to read his eyes. She wanted to know that he wasn't trying to hide his disappointment or uncertainty. Shirley needed Garrison to wrap her in one of his bear hugs that melted away all her worries.

While Garrison and the rest of the citizens of Charleston were enjoying their gifts, families, and Christmas dinner tomorrow, who knew where she'd be? When she found the last ornament—if she found it—who would know? How could she come this far and not share the moment with the people she cared for the most? Shirley wanted more than ever for Garrison to be by her side.

"I'll have to catch up with you later," he had said hurriedly, hanging up the phone before she had a chance to respond.

Shirley practiced a calming technique, taking deep breaths through her nose and exhaling through her mouth, relieving the stress she felt building in her temples.

"Is that what you're wearing?" Her mother snapped the clasp closed on her purse when Shirley entered the room.

"What's wrong with what I'm wearing?" Shirley asked. Black pants. Cream turtleneck.

"Well, no offense, but you look like you're an usher at a theater. Something at bit jazzier might be nice."

"Hmm. Jazzier? If you say so."

Shirley wasn't in the mood to play tug-of-war with her mother. Besides, she had to admit Mama was right. She did look bland for the occasion. Shirley went into her bedroom, dug around in the back of her closet for the jazziest ensemble she could find, then emerged wearing a long-sleeve silver sequined blouse that clung loosely around a pair of green velvet pants. High heels would have topped the look off, but there was no way she'd be able to manage them the entire evening.

"Better?" She walked out into the living room and gave a twirl.

"Much better, and absolutely beautiful."

"Why are you looking at me like that?" Shirley put on a pair of teardrop earrings.

"Because I'm proud of you," Mama said. She clenched her mouth together and shook her head as if willing the tears not to fall.

Shirley pulled her mother into an embrace. "Don't start the waterworks. You know it's hard to turn off for the both of us." She squeezed her one last time before letting go. "We should get going since we need to scoop up Dot."

"You wouldn't want to be late on a special day like this," Mama said, picking up her fur-lined hat.

It was Shirley's first time seeing the Christmas tree festival under the evening sky in the atrium, and the sight was spectacular. The decorated trees boasted a unique charm that reflected the beauty of their beloved city, and it further affirmed Shirley's decision to return to her hometown. Living in Charleston brought out all the best parts of her.

"This is magnificent," Mama said, her mouth agape in awe, the same as Dot's. They looked like children who were seeing the magical lights of Christmas for the first time. Shirley had to capture the moment.

"Scoot over, Mama," Shirley said. "Now get close to Dot. I want to take a picture. This will be a good one for your new photo album."

The elderly ladies leaned in close, their arms around each other and their temples touching. Shirley felt blessed knowing they had each other during this time of their lives. They'd formed a new outlook on life. Regardless of their age, they were determined to squeeze as much happiness out of their remaining years as they could. They'd even had discussions about how they wanted to celebrate their centennial birthdays, though both were over a decade away.

"Make sure you get a copy of that printed out for me," Dot said. "These days everyone's pictures are stuck in their phone."

"Yes ma'am," Shirley promised.

She left her mother and Dot to wander through the atrium, taking in all the sights. Everyone seemed to be enjoying themselves. Shirley had been unsure about the turnout of an event on Christmas Eve, but it had generated a larger crowd than she had expected. The jubilation was palpable. There was no place Shirley would rather be tonight, and it seemed most of the employees and their families shared the same sentiment.

Shirley spotted Garrison across the lobby and waved to get his attention. Their eyes met, albeit briefly. He smiled at her but disappeared in the growing crowd and the wave of people who had just entered the building.

Maybe he's still taking care of that emergency, Shirley thought. They'd connect sooner or later. She tried to be present in the moment, but the words of her last clue kept pushing to the front of her mind.

To the place where it all began, the years ahead are blessed. Underneath her gaze and an open sky, if only you'll say yes.

Shirley had come too far to give up now. She looked around at the people who were silently depending on her. She thought about the patients who had yet to step foot into the halls of Mercy Hospital, who would benefit from the capital upgrades, latest medical technologies, and health care programs.

When Shirley had the opportunity to briefly glance through the proposals that had landed on Garrison's desk, she'd noticed one from Kaye, who wanted to establish a music therapy program to enhance care in the hospital. Shirley hoped that one passed successfully through all the red tape.

And there she is now, Shirley thought as Kaye pushed her way through the crowd to her with the rest of the chorale following behind—including Buddy. They were dressed in white sweaters with red and green plaid scarves draped around their necks.

"Thank you for including Buddy," Shirley said. "A little kindness goes a long way."

"And some creative thinking does too," Kaye said. Her smile didn't crack when she confessed, "Everyone's mic will be turned on except his. We've worked it all out with the audio guy."

"Oh." Shirley's eyes widened. "Ohhhhhh."

"He's none the wiser," Kaye said, satisfied. "Excuse us if you will. We need to go warm up."

"Good luck," Shirley said, noticing Garrison across the room again. He pulled his phone from his pocket, looked to be sending a text message, then shoved the phone back in his pocket when Julie approached him. He listened to her intently. Whatever was happening, Julie would help him handle it. She always did.

Shirley felt the same way about Joy, Anne, and Evelyn. If there was anything that needed to be handled, she could depend on them to be by her side.

Before she realized it, her friends had surrounded her.

"We're concerned about that expression we saw on your face from way over there," Anne said.

"Yes. You look like you have something on your mind," Evelyn added.

She didn't want to hide her true feelings from her friends. Even if she tried, they would read right through her.

Shirley attempted to put on a strong countenance but she felt the tears well in the corners of her eyes. "I was thinking about all the things we've been through this year and how I'm blessed to have you all in my life. I wouldn't have gotten this far without you, and I mean it from the bottom of my heart."

"Oh, Shirley, you know we're a bunch of softies when it comes to each other. If you start the waterworks with us, I'm afraid we won't stop."

Shirley wiped away her tears of joy as Aurora whisked by.

"Hurry, ladies. Come and get your hot cocoa for the toast. I want you all front and center. As a matter fact, follow me."

Shirley apologized to the people she skipped as Aurora pushed them to the front of the line. Servers were lined along the cocoa stations, dropping in teaspoons of sweets and candies. Shirley asked for marshmallows, crushed peppermints, and caramel morsels, which she stirred with a spoon.

Five minutes later, the growing jangle of jingle bells filled the atrium, and the administrators stepped up on the dais, ushered in by the voices of the Mercy Christmas Chorale. Shirley couldn't help but chuckle at the sight of Buddy as he belted out the tune of "Winter Wonderland," not knowing that he and those closest were the only ones who could hear him.

"Merry Christmas Eve, everyone." Paula from the public relations department started her opening remarks. "Someone asked me yesterday, wouldn't I rather spend my Christmas Eve with family instead of coming to Mercy Hospital? I told them that Mercy *is* my family."

Applause erupted. The joyous scene warmed Shirley's heart as she and the staff and employees around her encircled each other with hugs and smacked high fives. Shirley felt a hand on her back. She looked over her shoulder to smile at Garrison. Except it wasn't him. It was her mother who had somehow pushed her way to the front, balancing a cup of cocoa.

Paula continued once the noise subsided. "We've gathered today to celebrate not only the culmination of Mercy's Festival of Christmas Trees but to toast to the wonderful work we've accomplished at Mercy Hospital. Our nearly two-hundred-year history has brought us to this point, and our foreseeable bright future will continue to carry us. Every person who has ever walked the halls of Mercy Hospital—whether it be thirty years, thirty days, or three weeks ago—has left an indelible impression that will never be erased."

Shirley was surprised that Garrison hadn't made it to the dais. She craned her neck to see if she could catch a glimpse of him among the crowd. She scoured the faces to her right and left, but he was nowhere to be found.

"We're thankful to all of you and pray that God blesses you in a special way this Christmas as we celebrate the birth of the Savior."

Paula turned around and accepted a steaming cup from one of the servers behind her. "We raise our cups to the past. We raise our cups to the present. We raise our cups to the future. Merry Christmas, everyone."

Shirley took a cautious sip of her cocoa, though it had cooled to the point that she didn't need to. She turned, intending to speak to her mother but walked into Garrison's chest instead. He slid the cup of cocoa from her hand and gave it to Joy, then gripped her hand and guided her through the crowd.

She looked back at her friends, who seemed to be just as stunned as she.

"Where are we going?" Shirley asked him, though she doubted he could hear her over the rumbling of voices and the Mercy Christmas Chorale that had begun to sing again. He slowed down their pace once he pushed open the doors that led out to the Grove.

Garrison and Shirley walked hand in hand until they reached the Mercy Angel statue. It seemed to glow from the reflections and shimmer of the twinkling lights from the Christmas tree beside it.

"Garrison, what's happening? I thought you were dealing with an emergency."

"I am," he said. He took off his coat and wrapped it around Shirley's shoulders. "I was trying to think if there was a way that I could live without you."

"What? Garr—"

Garrison touched a finger to her lips. "And I realized that I can't. And I don't want to."

They stood alone under the canopy of clouds and stars with nothing but their love and future between them. Garrison reached up to a branch on the Christmas tree and pulled off a single silver ornament, hidden among the large red bulbs. Shirley shivered, though she knew it wasn't from the dipping winter temperatures. Tears welled in her eyes, which Garrison brushed away.

He knelt on one knee. "My life changed the moment I laid eyes on you. I knew you were special. I knew it would take a while to chip away at the wall you'd built to protect your heart. And I was willing to wait for however long it would take. And if you would allow me to be your husband, you won't have to protect your heart again. Because I will."

Garrison flipped a clasp on the ornament and opened the hinged top to reveal the most beautiful diamond ring Shirley had ever seen.

"'To the place where it all began, the years ahead are blessed. Underneath her gaze and an open sky, if only you'll say—'" Garrison stared into Shirley's eyes.

A lump caught in her throat. She had memorized those exact words over the last two days. She'd played them in her mind repeatedly, never realizing they'd be the words that would change her life.

"Yes," Shirley whispered, as he slipped the ring on her finger. It was the perfect fit, just like Garrison was the perfect fit for her. She laughed uncontrollably as he swept her off her feet and spun her around. "Yes! Yes! Yes!" She wrapped her arms around his neck and held on for what felt like forever.

When Garrison gently set her back on her feet, she could see that he was crying too. He always carried a handkerchief in his back pocket. He pulled it out and mopped his face.

"There's one more thing."

Shirley had been so caught off guard by Garrison's proposal she hadn't noticed the gold box under the tree. He held it out and opened the top, letting her lift the ornament.

The Mercy Angel. Shirley held it up to the shimmering Christmas tree lights and placed it on the highest branch she could reach. And then out of nowhere, she noticed lights moving slowly in her direction, almost as if they were floating in the air.

Shirley wiped away the rest of her tears and focused on what was happening before her. Friends, colleagues, and family came into vision, carrying candles that flickered inside of glass globes. They formed a circle around her and Garrison. Her mother and Dot. Anne and Ralph. Evelyn and James. Joy and Roger.

As the circle closed in tighter, Shirley noticed the colleagues who'd worked by her side for almost the last two years. Paige, the head nurse in pediatrics. Dr. Barnhardt. Dr. Perez from obstetrics. Aurora. Julie. Now her tears streamed like waterfalls, heavy and unlimited. She spotted every person she'd encountered during the last month, from the woman waiting at the finish line of the 5K Hot Cocoa Run, to Abrielle and Claire from the Belina House Gallery and Luna from the animal shelter. Even Noelle and Nancy from the Charleston City Market with their hair in all its glory.

"I can't believe it," Shirley cried.

"Believe it," Garrison said, cocooning her inside of his arms. "Today marks the first day of the rest of our lives."

"So does this mean Mercy Hospital will receive the donation from Mr. Christmas?"

Garrison reached into the pocket inside of his suit coat and pulled out a gold envelope. Instead of handing it to Shirley, he flipped open the tab and pulled out a check made out to Mercy Hospital in the amount of twenty-five million dollars. She could tell from the thickness of the paper that the check wasn't real but was meant to be a representation of the funds to come.

When Garrison held the check in the air, the applause was so thunderous that Shirley couldn't hear what Garrison was saying in her ear. He then raised her left hand above her head to show off her diamond.

Shirley tilted her face toward the heavens. God had blessed her immensely. More blessings than she could count and more than she felt she deserved.

"Thank You, Lord, and thank you, Mr. Christmas," she whispered. Now it all made sense. This *was* the place of new beginnings.

When Garrison wrapped her in his arms again, Shirley could hardly believe that it would be her safe place forever. "I can't wait to marry you," she said.

"Then don't," Garrison said. "We can get married tomorrow. On Christmas Day."

"Garrison," Shirley said, pushing back so she could stare into his eyes, "you can't be serious."

"I've never been more serious," he said. "All you have to do is say the word, and I'll make it happen."

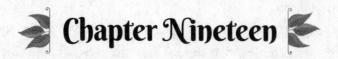

Chapter Nineteen

SHIRLEY HAD TO PINCH HERSELF on Christmas morning to make sure she wasn't in a dream. It was nothing she'd expected, yet everything she'd ever wanted. To think that she was engaged to Garrison put a smile on her face that hadn't left all day. Shirley believed her pear-shaped diamond had the same effect on her as Queen Victoria had on her mother. They were both unmistakably happy.

Shirley stood behind Garrison. Her gift to him was on his lap as he prepared to open it. Considering what was on her finger, she knew his gift paled in comparison, but there was no turning back now. Maybe her mother was right. Maybe she should have done something different.

He yanked the bow off before Shirley had time to give her semiprepared speech about why she'd chosen the gift.

"How did you know?" Garrison asked with a smile.

"How did I know what?" Shirley asked, her arms wrapped around his neck. "About you and Mr. Christmas playing checkers? You told me you did, and once I walked in on you two during a game."

"I remember that time you walked in on us," Garrison said. "I didn't know how long you had been standing there, and I was afraid you'd heard what we were talking about."

"You and Mr. Christmas were holding secrets, huh?" Shirley walked around and sat down beside him.

"We had a lot of heart-to-heart talks while we played. That's what it was really about. Even more than the game, which he always spanked me in."

"I could tell during my brief interruption that you shared something special during that time. That's the reason I thought this checkerboard set would be a nice gift. I wanted to commemorate your time together and your relationship. Not to mention, it looks almost exactly like the one Mr. Christmas had."

"Nearly identical," Garrison said. He lifted the top of the hand-carved box. The board and pieces inside were made of rich maple and walnut woods. The heavy grain would last long enough for him to pass the set down through generations if he desired.

"What you don't know is that when you walked in on us, we were talking about you. We talked a lot about life and marriage. He knew I was planning to propose, and he wanted to help me make it something special. He insisted that he use the last clue to bring you to the Mercy tree for the proposal."

"So it's your fault I was running around Charleston during Christmas," Shirley said, playfully punching him.

Garrison held his hands up in defense. "I didn't know all the details, but I admit I didn't consider the added stress it might cause. I thought it would be different."

"It was different all right."

Queen Victoria barked from the throne she'd been sitting on all morning—her mother's lap. Mama laughed and rubbed the top of Queen Victoria's head. "The Queen agrees."

"Mr. Christmas told me to trust him. He knew he wouldn't live to see it, but he said his assistant would bring me a copy of the clue when it was almost time so I could plan everything perfectly. It couldn't have worked out better."

Shirley couldn't help but pry for more answers. "So everyone who was there knew about the proposal the entire time?"

"Of course not. They didn't know until they were given the candle before coming outside. Julie helped me with all of that. You know she's efficient and a stickler for details."

"I'm the only one he told about the proposal," her mother said proudly. "And also, as a man who has been raised well, he came over one day to ask for permission for your hand in marriage. I told him the sooner the better."

They shared a laugh.

"Those were actually her exact words," Garrison said.

Shirley held her hand in the air and twisted her wrist. The gleam of her engagement ring caught the Christmas morning sunshine.

"Well, there's one thing Garrison didn't tell you," Shirley said to her mother with a sly smile. She entwined her fingers through her fiancé's. "We're getting married today."

Mama sat up abruptly in her chair, looked at the two of them, and then slouched back down. She patted the top of Queen Victoria's head. "Oh, you two need to stop playing with me. It's Christmas, not April Fool's Day."

"It's not a trick," Garrison assured her with a wide grin. "It's our gift to you. The sooner the better, right? You said so yourself."

Shirley could practically see the wheels in her mother's head begin to spin.

"How in the world can you make that happen? There's too much to do. Why, I'm mother of the bride and I don't have a dress. Shirley doesn't even have a wedding dress."

"Mama, you've always told me that marriage is not in the things. It's not even in the wedding. It's in building a life together with the person you love and keeping God at the center of it. Today may not look like all you've ever envisioned, but it will be all I've ever wanted. You and a strong, God-fearing man by my side."

"But what about Cynthia? She's all the way in California," Mama asked.

"Mama, you know with all this fancy technology, it will be just like she's right there with us. I don't know how Garrison has done it again, but he's pulled most of the pieces together in a matter of hours. Except for the marriage license, which he got last week. He must have been pretty sure of my answer." She laughed and squeezed his hand.

"I'm just glad I could apply for it online and keep it a surprise," Garrison said. "Fortunately, I had the info I needed in your personnel file."

Shirley kissed his cheek. "I won't report you to HR this time. And Mama, I'll go through your closet to help you find something to wear. I already have an idea in mind."

"This is really happening today?" Mama asked, disbelief all over her face.

Shirley got up and knelt in front of her mother. She grabbed both of her hands with hers. Garrison stood and walked over behind his future mother-in-law. He placed his hands on her shoulders and gave them a gentle squeeze.

"Today," Shirley said. "As the sun is setting, we'll become husband and wife."

And as the joy of Christmas morning turned into the peace of Christmas night, Shirley stood outside of the closed double doors leading into the sanctuary of Mother Emanuel, waiting to walk down the aisle. She closed her eyes, inhaled deeply, then exhaled slowly so her fluttering heart would calm. She wasn't uneasy or anxious in the least bit. She knew this was the right thing to do. At the right place. The right time. And definitely with the right man.

Shirley heard the soft whisper of one of her closest friends.

"I'll open the door whenever you're ready," Anne said. "Take as much time as you need."

The doors were the entrance into the next stage of Shirley's life, and some of the people she held dearly in her heart would be there to witness it. Her life looked different than it did over a year ago. She'd returned to Charleston with intentions to aid her elderly mother and continue to grow her nursing career in the halls of Mercy Hospital. Both of which she'd done. Those two things alone made her happy. But God had so divinely orchestrated beautiful relationships in her life—and one who she was about to vow her life to forever. Today would be a Christmas she would never forget.

"I'm ready," Shirley said.

Anne opened the door, and the scene took Shirley's breath away. The ends of the sanctuary pews were decorated with teardrop garland and ivory satin ribbons. Ralph stood at the front of the aisle with Garrison by his side. His hands were clasped behind his back. He wore a simple but flattering tan suit with a red tie and a red rose boutonniere. It was a nice complement to Shirley's calf-length ivory evening dress. She'd originally worn it to a fundraiser gala at the previous hospital she'd worked at when living in Atlanta, but she'd never felt more beautiful in it than she did now.

She believed Garrison felt the same way. Their tears seemed to fall in sync as she approached the altar. He pulled a handkerchief from his pocket and dabbed her cheeks and the corners of her eyes.

"You look amazing," Garrison said to her.

They couldn't take their eyes off each other. Although Shirley knew Mama, Dot, Anne, Joy, Roger, Evelyn, and James were seated on the first rows, it felt like only the two of them. All the inhibitions she'd ever had about finding love had fallen away. Ralph led them through the sacrament of their wedding vows, and they partook in the Holy Communion.

In an act that neither Shirley nor Garrison had expected or requested, her mama closed out the ceremony singing "The Lord's Prayer." Her voice was soft, but the words and sincerity were so powerful that they moved everyone in the intimate ceremony to tears.

"In the presence of God, your family, and friends, I now pronounce you husband and wife. Garrison, you may kiss your beautiful bride."

Shirley beamed as she looked up into Garrison's eyes. In them she saw her father's strength, her mother's gentleness, and the Father's love. He pulled Shirley into his arms and kissed her with a passion that made her feel like she'd melt into him.

"I love you, Garrison," Shirley said.

"I love you, more, Mrs. Baker."

Dear Reader,

There's something about Christmas. The aroma of freshly baked cookies, pine from the live Christmas tree, and apple cider with cinnamon and orange slices warming in the slow cooker. The sight of twinkling white lights draped on bushes and the live Nativity scene in front of the local church as dusk settles. Christmas carols piping through store speakers and the children who ready their voices for the annual Christmas play. We pull on fuzzy socks, wrap in flannel blankets, and enjoy the warmth from the fireplace. Christmas has easily become one of the favorite times of the year for my family. Though my children are still young, I've noticed how they now focus less on gifts and more on memories, less on presents and more on presence.

I can only imagine (and one day hope to visit) the beauty of a Charleston Christmas, though definitely not in the same way that Mercy Hospital's beloved nurse, Shirley Bashore did! And for you—at Christmas—may you find everything you need, and more.

God's love and mine,
Tia McCollors

About the Author

ALTHOUGH TIA MCCOLLORS ONCE DREAMED of being a TV network news anchor, her love of books and her writing talent led her in a different direction. Following graduation, she built a successful career as a public relations professional for nearly a decade, but the desire to write books was always calling her name. She listened and began writing her first novel on a yellow legal pad with pencil in hand.

Eighteen years later, Tia still finds joy in crafting novels that not only entertain readers but draw them into a closer relationship with God. To date, Tia has written twelve novels and one nonfiction devotion book, has been published in various online communities, and has become a regular contributor for the Women of Color Devotional and the *Daily Guideposts* devotion compilations.

When she's not writing, Tia spends her time choosing paint colors and redoing floor plans for the latest renovation project with her husband, and shuffling her three children to band, cheerleading, football, and track practices. Of all the stories she's written, she hopes the greatest story ever told is the life she's building with her family.

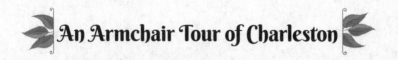

An Armchair Tour of Charleston

The Charleston City Market

THE CHARLESTON CITY MARKET is home to over fifty Gullah artisans and has also become the center of sweetgrass basketry. The tradition of sweetgrass basketry in Charleston dates back more than three hundred years but originated in West Africa, where they were constructed as winnowing fans used to separate rice seed from its chaff. What was once a necessity for labor has become a sought-after souvenir for visitors.

A group affectionately known as the "basket ladies" is located at the Charleston City Market. Their art has been passed down throughout the generations and doesn't involve the typical technique of weaving but using a specific coiling method. The baskets are woven using sweetgrass, palmetto frond, and pine needles.

The original Centre Market was constructed in 1807 on land that was ceded to the city in 1788. Following several stages of construction, surviving a tornado and also a fledging economy, it began to regain popularity in 1973 after being placed on the National Register of Historic Places. The early 2000s brought a multimillion-dollar makeover to the Charleston City Market, and the newly refurbished market opened in the summer of 2011.

Good for What Ails You

Low Country Boil

Also known as Frogmore Stew, it's a South Carolina favorite. Grab a pot, and let's get cookin' this flavorful meal rooted in the tradition of Gullah culture.

Ingredients:

3–4 ounces preferred seafood seasoning

4 pounds medium red potatoes

2 to 3 medium sweet onions (peeled and cut into quarters)

2–3 pounds cured, smoked pork sausage links

4 pounds medium shrimp

8–10 ears of corn, halved

2 halved lemons

Directions:

- Fill a 7-gallon stockpot halfway with water and add seafood seasoning. Bring to a rolling boil.
- Add potatoes and return to a boil. Cook 5 minutes.

- Add peeled and quartered onions along with pieces of smoked pork sausage links. Bring water back to a boil. Cook 10 minutes, making sure potatoes are done.
- Finish by adding shrimp and corn. Bring water back to a boil. Cook until the shrimp turn pink. This may take 3 to 5 minutes.
- Avoid overcooking ingredients.
- Drain all ingredients through a colander.
- Serve with lemon on newspaper.

Other alternative ingredients: chicken thighs, lobster tails, crab legs, mushrooms, garlic.

Serve with garlic bread, butter, cocktail sauce, sour cream, salt, and pepper.

*Read on for a sneak peek of the first book in
an exciting new mystery series from Guideposts Books—
Secrets from Grandma's Attic!*

History Lost and Found

BY BETH ADAMS

"Tracy?" Tracy Doyle's husband, Jeff, appeared in the doorway, silhouetted against the sunlight that streamed in through the over-sized front windows. "They're going to be here any minute." He tilted his head, as if trying to understand why she was sitting down.

"I know." Tracy sighed. It had been a long week, but there were still things that needed to be done before her sister, Amy, and her kids arrived for Matt's birthday party. First, she needed to put drinks in the tub of ice, then add the finishing touches to the Spider-Man cake. But Tracy had gotten distracted. She held Grandma Pearl's Bible in her hands, the pages worn soft with use. She'd recently found it in the attic, where well-meaning relatives had moved items from Grandma's bedroom after she'd passed. "I was just wondering about Jana and Matt."

"What about Jana and Matt?"

"I never really paid attention to the family records pages in Grandma's Bible before, but I was looking up a verse to read to Matt tonight and saw it in there, and that got me to thinking." She indicated the "Births" page, which was carefully filled out in peacock-blue ink. "I was wondering when we should add them to the family tree."

Grandma Pearl had carefully recorded each member of the family, starting with her great-grandparents. She'd also written the date of her own marriage and the birth dates and marriages of each of her children and grandchildren. There was Tracy's name, with her birthday recorded in Grandma Pearl's sure hand, and the date she'd married Jeff, as well as the birthdays of their kids, Chad and Sara. Her cousin Robin's birth and marriage were there, as was the birth of her son, Kai. And there was Amy. She'd never married, but her two foster children had quickly became family.

"Maybe it's best to wait until the adoption is finalized," Jeff said.

Tracy knew that was the logical answer. Jana and Matt felt like family, but they weren't yet—not officially, anyway. Their adoption still had to work its way through the Missouri legal system before it would become final. But Amy loved them like they were born to her.

"You're probably right," Tracy said. She started to push herself up, but then she noticed something else on the page.

"What?" Jeff was watching her, his eyes narrowed.

She didn't answer right away. She looked down at the page, trying to understand. She was reading it correctly. But it made no sense.

"Grandma listed each of her children," Tracy said. "Ruth, Abigail, and Noah."

"Right…"

"But there's a fourth name here. Ezekiel Collins."

"Under your grandmother's name?" Jeff stepped forward.

"Yes. Under her and Grandpa. Just like he's another one of their children. But who in the world is Ezekiel Collins?"

Did Tracy have an uncle she'd never heard of? But how was that possible? Why would Grandma or Grandpa never have mentioned him? And yet there he was, recorded in Grandma's Bible in Grandma's handwriting. It couldn't be a mistake.

"That's strange," Jeff said, studying the page. But before he could say anything more, the doorbell rang. A second later the door opened, and Jana and Matt ran into the house and right through the parlor to the living room, where a stack of birthday presents waited. Tracy heard screeching as the children saw the gifts.

"They've decided they don't need to act like guests," Amy said, stepping in behind them. Jeff followed the kids into the living room and was already riling them up, urging them to guess what was inside each box.

"They're absolutely right," Tracy said. She closed the Bible and walked over to the front door and pulled her sister into a hug. "How are you?"

"I'm fine. The kids are a little bit excited."

"As they should be. It's not every day a boy turns ten."

Amy pulled back, and Tracy saw that her sister had dark circles under her eyes and her hair was past due for a trim. But she looked happy. Raising two active kids would do that to you.

"Matt told me on the way over that this is the first real birthday party he's ever had."

"That's really sad." The news hit Tracy like a punch to the gut.

"It's awful, isn't it?" Amy shook her head. "Their birth parents… Well, I imagine they did the best they could under the circumstances."

Amy was being charitable. Tracy didn't know the full story, but she understood that drugs had played a part in how Jana and Matt ended up in foster care.

"Thank you for doing this."

"Now I'm sorry I'm not doing more. This is just a family party. If I'd known that, I would have invited his whole class and rented a bouncy house and hired a clown and—"

"Clowns are creepy. This is perfect, Trace. Thank you." Amy looked down at the Bible that was still in Tracy's hands. "Doing some light reading?"

"Something like that." And then, after a pause, she said, "Hey, have you ever heard of someone by the name of Ezekiel Collins?"

Amy's brow wrinkled. "I don't think so. Who is he?"

"He's listed here in Grandma's Bible." Tracy opened to the records page and showed it to Amy.

"What in the world?" Amy looked up, her eyes wide. "Do we have an uncle we never knew about?"

"It kind of looks like that's what this means."

"How is that possible?" Amy asked.

"Can we open the presents now?" came a cry from the living room.

"Not yet," Amy called back. "You have to wait until your cousins get here."

"When will they get here?" Jana asked on Matt's behalf.

"Soon," Amy called. Then, to Tracy, she said, "When will they get here?"

"Soon." Tracy smiled. Chad and Sara were coming with their families, and Robin and her family would be here shortly as well. Tracy decided to put the question about Ezekiel out of her mind for now. She had an excited ten-year-old ready to enjoy his first birthday party ever. She needed to focus on him.

Tracy walked toward the bookshelves that lined the far wall of the parlor. Grandma Pearl had loved books, and the shelves were filled with hardcover editions of the classics as well as newer fiction, history, biographies, and a whole shelf of Christian titles. Tracy hoped to read through the entire collection someday. But that day would likely be far in the future, the way things were going. She bent down and set Grandma Pearl's Bible on the shelf. She'd focus on Matt now and worry about Ezekiel later.

Tracy had hoped to sleep in Saturday morning after the big party the night before, but the birds outside her window woke her with the sun. It was going to be a beautiful June day—she could already tell as she climbed quietly out of bed. Jeff could sleep through anything and would probably stay in bed for another hour at least. She padded down the creaky staircase into the kitchen and started the coffee.

They had been renovating Grandma Pearl's Victorian home since they'd inherited it. Bit by bit, they were scraping off decades of wallpaper, retrofitting bathrooms, and realigning floors, uncovering all kinds of secret nooks and crannies hidden behind haphazardly constructed walls in the process. The kitchen was the room

Tracy insisted they tackle first, and the big windows, gleaming white cabinets, and smooth granite-topped island still made her happy, every morning.

As the coffee brewed, Tracy fed their goldendoodle, Sadie, and spent some time reading her Bible and talking with the Lord. Then, fresh coffee in hand, she set about making her list of Saturday morning chores. There was laundry to do. And the bathrooms could use a good cleaning. She needed to vacuum after last night's party. Her library book was overdue. It had been a busy week at the newspaper, and with the party to prep for, she wasn't as on top of her to-do list as she would normally be. Then, there was the faculty lunch at the dean's house she and Jeff had to attend. And she'd promised Jeff she'd stop by the hardware store to get stain to refinish a dresser he'd found in the attic.

But even as she wrote, her mind kept drifting back to the name she'd found in the Bible last night.

Who was Ezekiel Collins?

Was Collins a middle name or a surname? If a surname, why would his be different than the rest of the Allen family? Had he died at birth and never been mentioned? What if he had run away or disgraced the family and been disowned? But Grandma would never do that. And Tracy's father would have surely mentioned him at some point. She couldn't figure it out. If she had another uncle, wouldn't she know about him?

Then Tracy had an idea. She glanced at the clock over the stove. The library would open shortly, and she needed to return her book anyway. She might not have the slightest clue who Ezekiel Collins was, but someone knew. There must be a record of him somewhere. And the Canton Public Library would be the best place to start.

Tracy made herself toast and eggs, and by the time she went back up the stairs to get dressed, Jeff was getting ready for his morning run. She'd never understand how that man could hop out of bed and go off and run three miles, but he did it almost every day.

"I'm headed to the library," she said, and he nodded, unsurprised. She did spend a lot of time there, she supposed. Jeff adjusted his earbuds and waved before he left. She dressed quickly and went downstairs, and then she walked out onto the porch and into the beautiful day.

The sun was warm on her skin, and the magnolias and primroses were in full bloom. Just before she climbed into her car, she looked back up at the house. It really was a gorgeous old Victorian, with its tall turret and generous front porch shaded by mature poplars and maples. Sometimes she still couldn't believe she got to live here.

She backed slowly out of the driveway. Tree limbs heavy with fresh green life arched over the street, shading the lovely old homes as she drove. Lewis Street was bustling, the sidewalks crowded with people enjoying the warm day. There was a line outside PJ's, as there was most days when his biscuits and gravy was on the menu. PJ kept saying he was going to remodel and add more tables, but Tracy knew that half the reason people came was for the battered wooden tables and booths that had been there for a hundred years. Robin's antique shop, Pearls of Wisdom, was open, and Jeannie's new bookshop looked to be doing a brisk business. Tracy was glad. Jeannie had worked so hard to rebuild after the fire, and now the shop was better than ever. She passed the newspaper office where she worked part-time during the week, and then the florist and coffee shop.

There were plenty of parking spots outside the library, which was housed in a historic brick building downtown. Tracy stepped inside, heading for the computer terminals. She returned her library book and waved at Grace Park, the head librarian, who was seated behind the checkout desk. As an investigative reporter, Tracy was very familiar with the research tools available at the library. She would start by searching their collection of newspaper archives.

"Hi, Tracy." Pastor Gary Bennett walked up to her, his two young grandchildren in tow. He always looked so formal when he was preaching, with his suits and ties, but right now, he just looked like a proud grandpa.

"Hello, Pastor." She glanced at the group of parents and toddlers gathering in the children's section. "Story time?"

"Indeed." He laughed. "And you look like you're on a mission."

"I am, I suppose," she said. Then she paused. Pastor Gary had been around Faith Chapel for decades. He'd been very close with Grandma Pearl. If anyone would know who Ezekiel was, Pastor Gary would. "I'm actually hoping to find out who Ezekiel Collins is—or was."

He recognized the name—that was clear. He startled, and his eyes widened.

"What makes you want to look into Ezekiel Collins?" he asked. His youngest grandchild, Henry, tugged on his hand.

"I found his name in Grandma Pearl's Bible." She watched as he shifted his weight from one foot to the other. "Do you know who he is?"

The words hung in the air just a bit too long before he answered.

"I don't," he finally said. "But I have to admit, Ezekiel Collins is a name that I've long wondered about."

Tracy wanted to ask a thousand questions, but she stayed quiet, waiting for him to go on.

"I have no idea who he is," Pastor Gary continued. "But he sends a sizable check to the church every month. I'd sure love to know who he is and why he sends that money."

A Note from the Editors

WE HOPE YOU ENJOYED ANOTHER exciting volume in the Sweet Carolina Mysteries series, published by Guideposts. For over seventy-five years, Guideposts, a nonprofit organization, has been driven by a vision of a world filled with hope. We aspire to be the voice of a trusted friend, a friend who makes you feel more hopeful and connected.

By making a purchase from Guideposts, you join our community in touching millions of lives, inspiring them to believe that all things are possible through faith, hope, and prayer. Your continued support allows us to provide uplifting resources to those in need. Whether through our online communities, websites, apps, or publications, we strive to inspire our audiences, bring them together, and comfort, uplift, entertain, and guide them.

To learn more, please go to guideposts.org.

Find more inspiring stories in these best-loved Guideposts fiction series!

Mysteries of Lancaster County

Follow the Classen sisters as they unravel clues and uncover hidden secrets in Mysteries of Lancaster County. As you get to know these women and their friends, you'll see how God brings each of them together for a fresh start in life.

Secrets of Wayfarers Inn

Retired schoolteachers find themselves owners of an old warehouse-turned-inn that is filled with hidden passages, buried secrets, and stunning surprises that will set them on a course to puzzling mysteries from the Underground Railroad.

Tearoom Mysteries Series

Mix one stately Victorian home, a charming lakeside town in Maine, and two adventurous cousins with a passion for tea and hospitality. Add a large scoop of intriguing mystery, and sprinkle generously with faith, family, and friends, and you have the recipe for *Tearoom Mysteries*.

Ordinary Women of the Bible

Richly imagined stories—based on facts from the Bible—have all the plot twists and suspense of a great mystery, while bringing you fascinating insights on what it was like to be a woman living in the ancient world.

To learn more about these books, visit Guideposts.org/Shop